Christmas 2005,
love michelle x

BRITAIN
What a State

Dedicated to every citizen of Britain.
And that includes you.

BRITAIN
What a State

A User's Guide to Life in the UK

Ian Vince

BⒾXTREE

First published 2005 by Boxtree
an imprint of Pan Macmillan Ltd
Pan Macmillan, 20 New Wharf Road, London N1 9RR
Basingstoke and Oxford
Associated companies throughout the world
www.panmacmillan.com

ISBN 0 7522 25987

9 8 7 6 5 4 3 2 1

A CIP catalogue record for this book is available from
the British Library.

Design by Ian Vince

Printed by Bath Press

Images in this book are by the author or from the author's private
collection. Other images are supplied by www.absolutvision.com,
Shutterstock Inc at www.shutterstock.com and the Jupiterimages
Corporation websites at www.photos.com, www.clipart.com and
www.photoobjects.net.

Acknowledgments

A government department like ours simply can't complete a project like this without the support and understanding of departmental aides, under-secretaries, friends and families.

First of all, thanks to our steering group, the Committee of Officially Sanctioned Words and Punctuation. Without their sterling work of dotting the 't's and crossing the 'i's, this book would have possibly taken half the time, but it was a simple misunderstanding and the Department is quite sure that everyone will be enjoying their new careers as soon as they obtain them.

Thanks also to Ms Natalie Jerome, Richard Milner, Esq. and assorted other fine folk at Boxtree and Macmillan. Also to the Department of Social Scrutiny's agent in the world of the creative marketplace, Simon Benham, Esq. Thanks are due in particular for all their magnificent work steering a huge department through the labyrinthine world of publishing. Your OBEs await you. Quite possibly. Just give it a year or two.

Copy-editing and indexing duties were performed for the Department by Richard Rosenfeld, Esq. who will now be elevated to the peerage as a member of the Hyphen, Golden Order of.

Ian Vince would like to thank his wife, Mrs Vince for her resilience, faith and understanding.

London, June 2005

Contents

Reader Satisfaction

Information

While we try to offer you a full
breakdown of the substance of
the book, the Contents page can
not guarantee that it is a full and
accurate representation of the
material on offer in the book, or
that it is a complete statement of
the topic matter or measure of
the general gist or pith available.

If this calming message has
failed to reassure, you may write
to us or to the Office of the
Contents Ombudsman, enclosing
a stamped, addressed envelope,
some paperclips, a tube of Pritt
Stick and some glitter for their
Blue Peter projects.

Before We Start

AN INTRODUCTION

CONTENTS

Introduction

By Alan Bladder, MP
Minister of Truth & Other Information

When I was asked to provide a foreword for this book – a few avuncular thoughts on nationhood and a cosy homily or two about the essential modesty of the British spirit – I thought very, very hard indeed before I finally said "No".

Because, in my experience of government, nothing could be that simple. Instead – and because it was a Tuesday – I arranged a series of strategic leaks and briefings against the book, accusing its author of Satanism and having an "unhealthy interest in the music of Val Doonican", before appearing on the *Today* programme to defend my position and, inevitably, challenge John Humphrys to a duel with flick-knives at dawn.

My department launched an official invest-igation into itself, sealing the fate of four "colleagues", all of whom are now forced to spend time with their dull families in order to save the government more embarrassment from their scurrilous counter-leaks implying I had somehow "changed my mind" and would write this fore-word after all. Utter bunkum.

This is a book about Britain, land of hope and glory, precious stone set in a silver sea, a green and pleasant land remarkable for its year-on-year sustained growth in light engineering as well as its very real potential for a strong footwear industry. Britain is both the cradle of polite, decent and rational society and the birth place of overseas exploration, two facts that led us to the realiza-tion that we are the oldest democracy in the

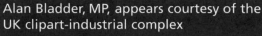

Alan Bladder, MP, appears courtesy of the UK clipart-industrial complex

world located in a temperate maritime climate, and that's something I'm immensely proud of.

And I'm proud of everything British. To me, Britain is the smell of a two-stroke petrol mower, the orderly stripe of a lawn and the snout of a mole twitching nervously from its burrow, catching the last precious drops of dew on a late Spring morning before it is dispatched with one blow of a spade manufactured in Sheffield.

However, not everybody sees Britain in precisely these terms and, in a spirit of national unity, it was decided to bring all British citizens into line with the government's views.

So it was that my colleagues at the Department of Social Scrutiny introduced the National Guide Book Bill into parliament – to produce this book, make its purchase and assimilation compulsory for every British citizen, and instill a sense of national pride into the population as a whole.

I do hope you enjoy reading this book, but in case you don't, I do hope you understand the penalties for not.

How to Use This Book

Guidance notes for successful reading.

Caution: Choking Hazard

Please keep this book out of the reach of gaping babies and children under 3, as an unusually wide mouth and a certain amount of infant determination may turn this book into a choking hazard.

Caution: Belief Hazard

This book is not a toy. You should keep official publications away from minors as child-like straight talking and/or rogue perspicacity renders official text and documents utterly pointless.

Directions For Use

1 Make sure the book is conveniently positioned and that there are no obstacles in your line of sight, clearing any out of the way using the back of your hand, a machete or flatbed truck, as appropriate.

2 Open the book by levering the front cover away from the rest of the volume, describing a steady arc with the cover. You are now ready to read.

3 Once you have finished reading, close the book and place on a non-sloping surface where it can be found again, such as a table or the middle of the floor. There is no need to "log-off" or close windows. All this is automatically performed for you by the book.

4 Exercise extreme caution while reading. If you are reading this paragraph, but "hearing" words other than the words printed, you are either experiencing co-channel interference caused by adverse weather conditions, or are about to be ambushed by some kind of philosophical device.

Key
to conventions & symbols

This handbook uses a series of icons, signs, symbols and conventions in order to make the rapid uptake of facts easier and much more streamlined than would be the case if clarity of expression was not desirable, in particular, one formed from non-obfuscatory discourse.

Stop
Stop Right Now. Do not continue to read further than this point under any circumstances. Wait for your name to be called out by somebody in charge.

No
You are not allowed to be in this part of the book. Who do you think you are, eh? Now go and sit down and wait for someone in charge to call out your name.

You can't stay here
You've really done it now. You've made us sit up and take notice and that's the last thing you want, believe-you-me – an army of pen-pushing, form-flapping gits armed with your name and address and a grudge.

Sorry
We are currently experiencing high tea. We take your questions very seriously and your enquiry will be dealt with as soon as an operator becomes available.

About the Department of Social Scrutiny

Secretary of State for Social Scrutiny, Sir Edward Bicycle, outlines a new programme of work for the department with more responsibilities, including tax, benefits and counter-insurgency measures.

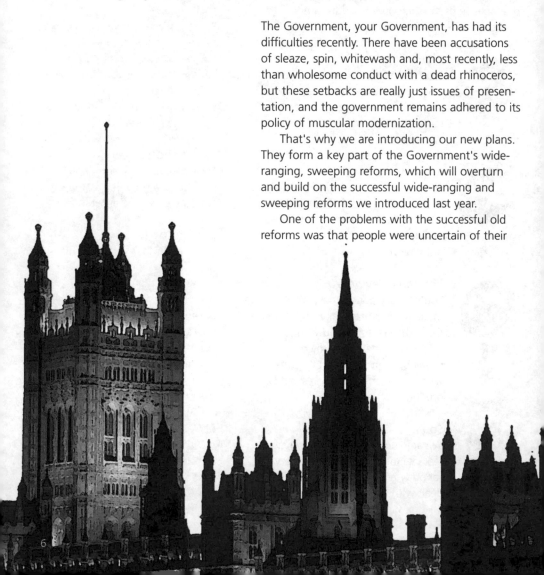

The Government, your Government, has had its difficulties recently. There have been accusations of sleaze, spin, whitewash and, most recently, less than wholesome conduct with a dead rhinoceros, but these setbacks are really just issues of presentation, and the government remains adhered to its policy of muscular modernization.

That's why we are introducing our new plans. They form a key part of the Government's wide-ranging, sweeping reforms, which will overturn and build on the successful wide-ranging and sweeping reforms we introduced last year.

One of the problems with the successful old reforms was that people were uncertain of their position within society. Furthermore, we are faced with the need to reformulate our, and by "our" I mean *your*, civil liberties in the context of a world where our, and by "our" I mean *my*, authority is under threat, and where that threat is clearly and without a shadow of doubt, you. We want to change that by screening the population and assigning you, the person, a position in society based on objective rules rather than wishy-washy ideas about aspiration and hope.

This new process includes this book, which you and every other citizen of this nation has been issued or, rather, been urged to purchase in order to avoid frankly terrifying legal procedures.

After you have learnt the contents of this book off by heart, the next step in the process will involve a series of many short interviews to gauge your comprehension of the key British principle of fair play, as mitigated by an eager respect of authority. In turn, the interview will help us determine whether you are going to be trouble.

People attending from outside the Home Counties will be allowed into the application office after inspections for head lice. Applicants using foul language outside the context of a discussion about art will be issued with vouchers for oven chips, and asked to leave.

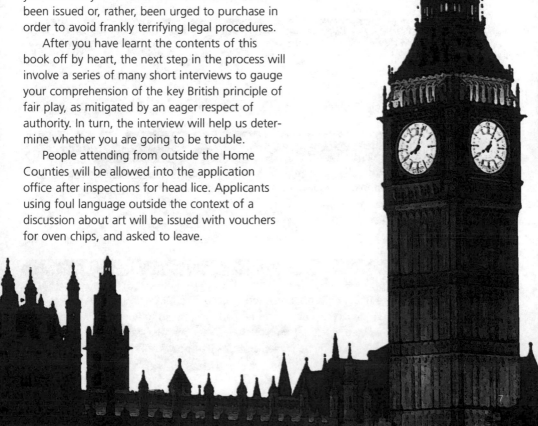

Serf Assessment

Before you begin to read this book, you must be classified according to a set of government benchmarks, which helps us to not only match you with potential employment, but also enables us to oppress you in a much more scientific and matter-of-fact manner.

We need to know: Do you own more reggae albums than is strictly necessary? Is your musky flat the habitat of a limp and feckless layabout? Do you wear the woozy, bloodshot gaze of a concussed spaniel? Do you often feel that you're just being too polite?

Or are you a thrusting and dynamic executive with good breeding and real potential for the island-hopping highlife? Do you ski, jetski, windsurf and fly aircraft? Do you want a job in Her Majesty's most exciting Service?

Are you a civil serf or a civil servant?

You are dimly aware that someone is following you in a car. Do you?

a Flag them down and offer them a lift as you're clearly heading in exactly the same direction. **0**

b Attempt to run them off the road by swerving around in your 1997 Nissan Micra. **2**

c Activate "Gazelle Protocol C" and garrotte them in a barn near Didcot. **5**

You hear a brief surge of white noise whenever you answer the telephone. Do you?

a Dry your ear, turn off the shower and answer the phone properly. **2**

b Phone MI5, witholding your number and disguising your voice by placing portions of satsuma in your mouth. **4**

c Blow up the telephone exchange with your specially adapted Argos fax machine. **6**

Your Caribbean beach holiday home is over-run by subversives. Do you?

a Offer to make a nice cup of chamomile tea to calm things down a bit. **0**

b Place everyone under citizen's arrest and wait for the fat villain to arrive to carefully explain his over-complex and flawed masterplan to you. **1**

c Escape to a nearby tool shed, from which you launch a devastating counter-attack with weapons fashioned from broken lawnmowers and plastic garden furniture. **4**

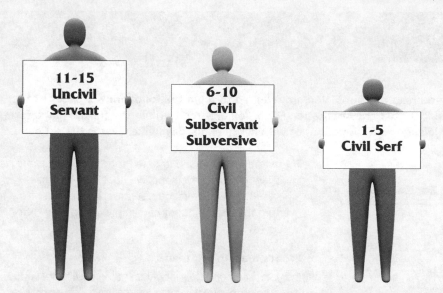

How did you score?

1-5 Civil Serf
Your innocence and naivety make you easy to keep tabs on – but, just in case, there's a radio transmitter implanted under one of your fillings.

That's all very well but you are still a credulous, compliant slave with a pathological inability to assert yourself in the face of the overwhelming power of the State. And don't think we don't appreciate it. It's people like you who make this country what it is.

6-10 Civil Subservant Subversive
On the one hand, you are obviously a little bit paranoid and flaky. But on the other hand, who wouldn't be when there's a man that lives under the stairs who records your phone calls and leaves subliminal messages made out of crumbs under the toaster?

Despite your fears, however, there is no question that you love your country, although this stems from a complete misunderstanding of the situation and is nothing to be proud of. Particularly in the light of the fact it's time to turn over the page and claim your National Identity Card.

11-15 Uncivil Servant
You've got it, baby we want it. You are a nasty piece of work – a faceless, shadowy, psychiatrically challenged festival of seemingly random violence. And that just turns us on.

By day, no one knows your true identity. By night, it turns out, you don't actually have one. But you can't hide from us for long. Come home, old thing: turn to page 106 for details of your first posting.

Before you read this book, you are required to fill in the following six pages of the National Identity Card Application Form. You are free to fill in the full 127-page form at your leisure, your discretion, or within 1 calendar day, whichever is the sooner.

These forms form a new updated form that reflects the important new improvements we have made to the scheme that were deemed to be necessary in order to overturn the old important new improvements we introduced last year.

What's it all about, then?

Insofarasisappropriate, notwithstanding exceptional and extenuating circumstances, the legal text that accompanies this form may consist of deeply obfuscatory compound Latin and portmanteau legalese pretend-word constructions designed to develop antagonistic neuralgia leading to weeks of nagging and unsatisfactory sleep. Heretwhich

andeverywhereinafter, you are advised to instruct a solicitor before you sign, or to take the advice of a suitably qualified professional, such as a friend of your sister who knew someone who was once followed home by a prowling member of the judiciary and, therefore, has an inkling of "how these things work".

Where do I start?

Please fill in the form carefully using black ink, block capitals and, except where indicated otherwise, an adult mental perspective uncluttered by your inner-fucking-child.

Fill in the form fully. If there is anything that you are not sure whether you should tell us, such as a deviant sexual fetish, membership of an underground organization or participation in a folk dancing society, please make a note of it on a separate sheet and mark your application "For the attention of the Arresting Officer".

National Identity Card Application Form

What if I don't tell you everything?

Failure to divulge information could lead to officially sanctioned harassment, legitimate paranoia and arrest that may, in turn, lead to imprisonment and compulsory viewing of Open University programmes.

In certain rare cases, imprisonment can lead to a chronic mental disfigurement such as a BA (Hons) in Town Planning or Psychology, as well as a degree of non-consensual buggery.

What if I don't understand?

DoSS is committed to serving the community, so if you find these forms difficult in any way, just call our Intelligence Impairment Unit and arrange a home visit, during which you will be spoken to in a loud, insistent voice and patiently stripped of your dignity.

What if I want to appeal?

Your request will be reviewed by a panel of spiteful paper-pushing automatons, while your benefit is with-drawn and members of your family are followed home, possibly by a prowling member of the judiciary. Your statutory rights are not effective.

What are the benefits?

Once issued, your ID card entitles you to full membership of Britain, including a full British Identity.

The British Identity is one of the most sought-after status symbols of the modern age. A veritable Rolls-Royce among inferior patriotic fixations, just being British equips you to stroll confidently around the world with a certain amount of overbearing gravitas and self-importance. Turn the page to begin right away.

Please fill in this form with a Medium 500μ Black Rollerball fineliner in BLOCK CAPITALS using a piece of lined paper underneath as a guide. You must answer ALL the questions. If you do not know the answer to a question you must think about it for a bit and make a pot of tea. The judge's decision is final.

Tick boxes (☐) should be filled in with a jaunty tick thus: ☑

Do NOT fill with a diagonal cross: ☒ This isn't the Football Pools.

Your name

Do you have a partner?
By partner, we mean someone you
habitually lie to, apart from us.

Yes ☐ Please send us some of their skin.

No ☐ Please tell us about your pathological
inability to trust others on a separate sheet.

May we look in your dustbin?
We need to do this in order to
freak you out.

Yes ☐ We will return in a suspect-looking boiler suit.

Do you have children?

No ☐ What have you done with them?

Yes ☐ Please answer the following question:

What is their total weight in bushels?
We need to know this in order to cause you
as much trouble as possible.

Bushels

Would you care for an older relative? No ☐ Thanks, I've just put one out.

Yes ☐ Please answer the following question:

Please estimate their calorific value

Kilojoules

Do you find this form confusing in any way? ☐ **9.** See 12 Across (4,3)

About your partner

Your name

That's a pretty name

About your ethical standpoint

Please explain your religion
eg, Feng-shui is not a belief system, it is merely a storage solution.

Please tick level of fervour
Religious mania is calibrated on an index of lateral quaking observed during theological debate. It runs from *light* (C of E Archbishop) to *beyond God* (Tony Blair).

C of E Archbishop ☐   Lapsed Clergy ☐

Smart Fridge ☐   Cliff Richard ☐

God ☐   Tony Blair ☐

Do you believe in miracles?

Since you came along. ☐ You sexy thing.

What is your view of xenophobia?

☐ It's a nice enough place but full of foreigners.

☐ I don't like spiders at all.

Would you lie on an official form?

No ☐

Yes ☐

What is your view on Justice?

☐ It works on criminals, but the innocent always seem to get away with it.

☐ It is quite the best furniture polish I have ever used.

How vegetarian are you?

☐ I refuse to eat animals that eat other animals.

☐ I eat free-range pebbles and polymerized tofu.

Do you partake in deviant sex?
By sex we mean mammalian intercourse with your partner or their slightly immoral and open-minded friend.

☐ Please explicitly elaborate on a separate sheet of tissue.

About your biometric data

- If your free, sterile pen pack is missing, please call the Department of Social Scrutiny's Special Pen Supply Section. At the main switchboard, ask to be put through to the Pen Pushers and await further dialling tone.

- Please fill in this form using only the pen provided and the appropriate genetic material. Wash your hands thoroughly, and apply the supplied hair net and face mask before removing the pen from its protective packaging.

- To prevent cross-question contamination occuring, you must microwave the pen for 30 seconds on full power between each answer. If you do not have a microwave, you should ask for the boil-in-the-bag version of this form.

Please provide an Iris Dump of your eye
Stand in strong light, holding the form 30cm from your face.
Stare at the black dot, until your eyes water. Do not blink.
Cross your eyes so that the blue circle contains the black dot.
Blink. The Iris Dump has been saved in a photo-chemical gateway in the white bullet point.

Please provide a DNA Sample
Please spit, bleed or ejaculate into the box.

Continue on a separate sheet, if required.

Please provide a lock of your hair
We need this in order to add it to our private collection.

Please gently brush it against your partner's ankle, and fix to the box provided.

If you carry any alien genetic code:

Are you in any way related to Sophie Ellis Bextor?

Please tick if you wish to be cloned

We will issue duplicate cards and partners.

About Your Majesty, Ma'am

- For the purposes of Royal Protocol, this form may be completed on behalf of One by One's Serf or Brown Nosing Lickspittle, Gawd bless you, Ma'am.
- If it would please Your Majesty, please do not staple any dead pheasants to this form.
- Completion of this document entitles the Majestic Applicant to 1 (one) Pointlessly Glorious and Gloriously Pointless State Jolly.
- Once completed, this form will withdraw from Your Majesty's presence backwards and face down to the strains of a popular Beatles song made lifeless, dreary and yet unnecessarily pompous by the Band of the Royal Marines.
- This form is also available in Imperial Measurements, Naval Semaphore and other anachronistic modes of measure and communication.

Your first twelve forenames

Previous surnames, aliases and false identities
Please list any names you were once known by
ie: Saxe-Coburg-Gotha, Da Riddim Masta, The Puppeteer, The Regal Bank Vole, etc.

Please use this box to paint your individual graffiti tag (watercolour or oils only, please)

Please plot your marital status on the dianacamillagram below:

Top Camilla.
Deemed unconstitutional.
Not Safe For Church.
Harmonious, yet somehow anodyne.
Horsey society girl / professional bachelor.
Wedding forms part of publicity brief.
Doomed sham.
Top Diana.

Path of Charles

Partners over relative time and infidelity

About Your Majesty, Ma'am

- Upon completion – and after the National Anthem has been dragged out for a mumble, like the tired old joke it is – if it pleases Your Majesty, One or a Member of One's Own Royal Gene Pool, may throw a bottle of fizzy wine against a sinister new government building, an anodyne memorial or a floating Death Machine of some kind.

BY APPOINTMENT TO HM THE QUEEN AND HER CONSORTIUM OF DULL, FECKLESS OAFS AND CHINLESS BUFFOONS. SUPPLIERS OF UNPARALLELED LUXURY AND A LIFE OF RILEY. APPARENTLY INFINITE TOLERANCE CO. OF GREAT BRITAIN.

Total number of imbecile children

One has a total of [ ] idiot spawn.

Items on One's Amazon Wish-List

[ ] Remaining third of Kent.

[ ] Gigantic fucking ship.

Serfs and nobs who work for One

[ ] Underlady of the Backstairs.

[ ] Lady Shaver of Gillette.

[ ] Tara Palmer Boom-de-ay.

[ ] Entire UK population.

Do you have any savings?

No [ ] Please see leaflet *About your girocheque.*

Yes [ ] Please communicate details of secret investments using cryptic display of half-mast flags, 21-gun salutes, One's Own motorcycle display team and Ascot head wear.

Britain: A Brief Outline
WHO, WHAT, WHERE, HOW AND WHEN

CONTENTS

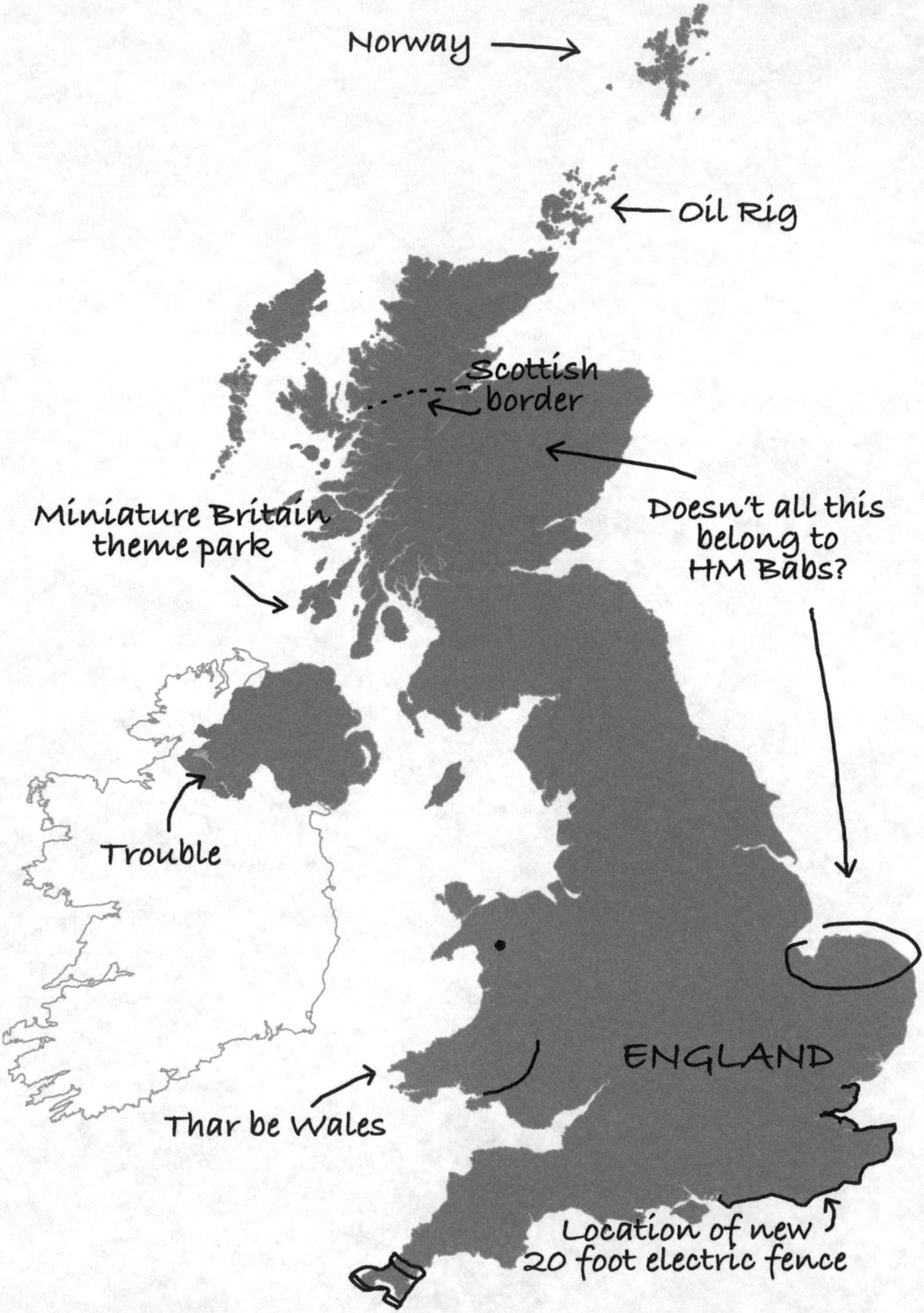

Norway →

← Oil Rig

Scottish border

Doesn't all this belong to HM Babs?

Miniature Britain theme park

Trouble

ENGLAND

Thar be Wales

Location of new 20 foot electric fence

Introduction

The United Kingdom is made up of four proud nations: England, Scotland, Wales and Northern Ireland, although we don't talk too much about the last one because it only causes trouble. Britain is, therefore, the only country in the world to be made of four other countries. These four nations are spread over a number of islands in the North Atlantic Ocean and, so far, most people are happy with the arrangement.

The four nations are further sub-divided into counties, boroughs, unitary authorities and districts, and are capable of alternating between different systems of local government virtually on demand.

It is a long-established tradition that local government reorganization – cited by many in power as one of their favourite hobbies – is good preparation for central government, where you inevitably spend a great deal of time altering constituency boundaries to maximize the number of your MPs in the next parliament. Drawing and re-drawing boundary lines until they work is seen as perfectly natural, though not officially sanctioned. This is why many Cabinet meetings are rounded off in darkened rooms, where ministers can secretly chop up lines and get their hands dirty by rearranging their members.

Britain? UK?

The Naming of the Parts

United Kingdom of Great Britain and Northern Ireland
Full name as notified to the World Bank for the purposes of keeping the bailiffs informed.

British Isles
England, Scotland, Wales, N. Ireland, Isle of Man, Channel Islands and the Isle of Sheppey.

Britain
England, Scotland and Wales.

Great Britain
England, Scotland and Wales, only better.

Briton
A fully British person.

Benjamin Britten
A tract of countryside in East Anglia that obsessively manufactures choral music.

The bits that Britain is made of
The Home Office Reminder Map of Britain, as amended and scribbled upon by successive Home Secretaries.

UK Facts

Form of Government
Constitutional Absurdity.

Currency
Cash, Boots gift tokens, sexual favours.

Language
The Queen's English – despite the fact that she is indisputably German.

Coastline
The coastline of Britain is 12,429 km (approximately 7,723 miles, 669 yds, 2 ft and $6^{13}/_{16}$ ins) long, but is fractal in nature and is, in fact, a little under infinite length at molecular level.

National Plant
The tree.

Atmosphere
Nitrogen 78%, oxygen 20%, laughing gas 1%. Trace elements include hallucinogen and the inert gas of tri-bellicose monomania.

Aside from the "Home Nations", the UK also has a number of overseas dependencies around the globe – former island colonies that are now used, principally, for parking the Royal Navy. Britain has spent the last 30 years turning shipyards and docks into scenic marinas and tourist attractions that seek to highlight the worrying loss of shipyards and docks, and the unsustainability of scenic marinas. And tourist attractions.

These days, the UK is technically a part of Europe, another – much larger – island to the southeast of Kent noted for its wine, food and meddling legislation. Currently, our official membership status is *in denial*. Recent unease about whether to become more involved in the activities of the Island of Europe have centred around the worry that most of the occupants of the offshore island appear to be foreign.

Politically, Britain belongs to a number of strategic international alliances including NATO, the UN, UNESCO, UNMOVIC and, lately, UNTIDY – the UN agency with special responsibility for not putting things back where they came from.

But Britain's international function is far more important. Though small,[1] its border surrounds the rest of the world it selflessly looks after.

Right: A fly pays the ultimate price for the sake of comparitive geographical scaling.

1. For example, if the world was represented by a grapefruit, Britain would be the approximate size of a housefly, firmly ground into the surface by a thumb the size of Brazil. Following the fly's compression, you could optionally use one of the wings to represent Eire, the Irish Republic of Ireland, but the remaining wing could be safely dispensed with.

Island Kingdoms

Not all of the islands around Britain's coast are part of the United Kingdom. Here are three that are not, as compiled by Her Majesty's Foreign Office.

The Isle of Man

Located in the Irish Sea, the island was originally purchased from Norway at an international car boot sale, but never fully accepted by the State.

The Isle of Man has its own parliament and laws, but it is probably most famous for the Manx cat. Represented on the Manx flag, the cat has no tail and only three legs and evolved from conventional domestic cats that were repeatedly run over by TT Race motorcycles.

The Isle of Wight

Though close to the mainland, treacherous seas and roaming cannibal tribes have laid to rest all hopes of an early colonization.

The Channel Islands

These have similar constitutional positions to the Isle of Man and, like the Manx, are represented by the UK internationally at pet shows and talent contests. Britain also has a defence agreement that allows sovereign islands like Jersey or the Isle of Wight to borrow its nuclear deterrent at weekends.

Interstellar Britain

Maps

Maps of the United Kingdom in this book are based upon the character of "Yukie, the Cuddly Yet Heavily Armed Country", and are reproduced here courtesy of the licensees, Anthropomorphic Industrial Behemoth, Inc.

Britain is a geophysicist's dream come true. And, although geophysicists are generally rather dull, they do become quite animated when confronted by the diversity and scale of the geology that created the UK. Indeed, as any geophysicist will breathlessly tell you, Britain is now recognized as the oldest country in the solar system since at least one part of Kent has now been proven to be formed from a small asteroid.

During the early days of the Earth's history, it was continually bombarded by meteors. These varied in size from tiny crumbs to large rocks that were the approximate dimensions of the Isle of Sheppey, including one that actually turned out to be the Isle of Sheppey. The discovery of Sheppey's part in the UK's evolution only proves the geophysicists' point that even a barren, lifeless rock with a poisonous atmosphere can have an interesting past.

Sheppey notwithstanding, the rest of Britain is made of terrestrial rock moulded by the same massive geological brute force responsible for pushing the Indian subcontinent towards Asia to form the Himalayas. In Britain, the Cotswolds were made the same way. They may not be as high – they are the result of the slow, polite and yacht-like collision of the Isle of Wight with Hampshire – but, as in so many other things in Britain, it is the taking part that counts.

Maidstone, we have a problem...

The Isle of Sheppey drifts towards Earth from deep space. Its new found home on the Thames Estuary makes Britain the oldest country in the solar system.

24

Divided by the Seaside

Apart from the venerable Isle of Sheppey (as detailed on the previous page), Britain, as we know it today, was formed somewhere in the Alps during the Ante-Histamine Era and was deposited at the snout of a glacier during the last Ice Age.

As water levels rose, Britain was lifted from its position on the Lap of Europe and carried 26 miles north to a sand bank, where it has been marooned ever since.

Now surrounded by sea, the UK has been subjected to countless millennia of coastal erosion and sedimentation. The sea has made us the shape we are, through a combination of processes so slow you can't help but wonder whether the Civil Service is involved. However, a much faster force is at work on the UK's coast: that of longshore drift, as shown in the facing diagram.

Longshore Driftologists (the science is young and a good name has yet to be decided upon) now calculate terrifying consequences if the drift goes unchecked, including a divided Britain, swivelling Ireland on its axis.

However, Leeds City Council – which stands to benefit from a new beach – is a little more optimistic. It has already produced a Leeds-on-Sea tourist brochure, and councillors have been spotted ferrying lorry loads of shingle to the mouth of the River Humber.

Britain's coastline today (inset) and in the future The ever-changing face of the UK and the disastrous consequences of longshore drift. As Britain is split along the Humber, the Kintyre peninsula pushes Ireland clockwise.

Before

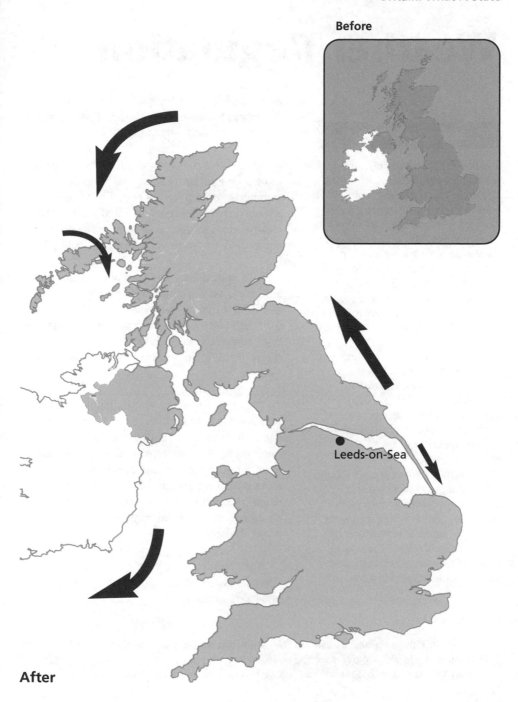

Leeds-on-Sea

After

Weather Regulation

Weather Talk

The British have a perennial fascination with the weather. In part this is because we have enough mildly interesting weather to make "changeable" an acceptable forecast for about 90% of the year, but it's also because the weather can sustain a conversation cycle for about 45 seconds – just enough time to peer into a stranger's psyche without involving any over-familiar emotional nonsense.

A typical exchange first sums up a current weather observation: "It's nice/awful/a bit wet isn't it?" A short discussion ensues about yesterday's weather as the participants seek to establish some kind of informal rapport.

In a crucial turn of the conversation – at a point when verbal gambits like "I tried to kill myself yesterday", or "Do you think my tits are nice?" hover as uneasy possibilities – the British offer "They say it's going to be warm tomorrow", and the moment of darkness passes.

British weather runs the gamut from mildly interesting to interestingly mild, but where does it all come from and why the south west?

These were the pressing questions that were to be answered by a parliamentary select committee formed for the purpose. In their interim report, MPs concluded that most British weather does indeed come from the south west and is carried here by wind from the south west.

MPs immediately saw the importance of wind and proposed a tougher regulatory framework for it. They felt that an over-reliance on weather from the south west was anti-competitive and weather from other suppliers, such as the north east, should be an integral part of the weather in the future.

Members urged year-on-year improvements to the weather to make it more interesting. They applauded the recent introduction of the hurricane to the climate, but felt there was no room for complacency and looked forward to more radical weather in the future. Members voted unanimously for less drizzle, though they did recognize it is an integral part of the identity of Manchester.

The committee then went on a series of fact-finding missions to investigate long periods of unbroken sunshine.

British sea areas, as used in the late night Radio 4 shipping forecast
The digital age will one day make the poetic murmuring of Chomsky, Spatula and Geronimo redundant, but the forecast will be retained for its tranquilizing qualities.

Shipping Areas

FINDUS

ROSS

BRRRRRRR

TEXAS

CACK

FRAY BENTOS

CHOMSKY

SPATULA

PENCIL

NEXT DOOR

GERONIMO

LUMBAR

BAUDRILLARD

J-LO

THE SEA

UNTITLED

DIRE STRAITS

WICKET KEEPER

FRANCE

SQUARE-LEG

SLIPS

Notable Events from the History of the Past

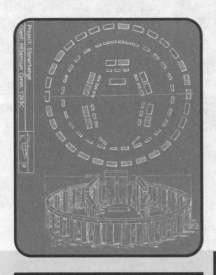

Do not stop reading. This chapter contains history that may excite feelings of pre-British nationalism. Make sure you leave enough time to exit the chapter safely.

It is often said that the past is a different country, and the Department of Social Scrutiny requires each and every Briton to pass through that country now, on your way to Britain – a journey of 5000 years from the first murmurings of consciousness to 1707, when England, Scotland and Wales became the entities they are today.

3100 BC	**Stonehenge constructed** Wiltshire County Council demand that retrospective planning permission is obtained.
55-54 BC	**Caesar invades Britain twice** First attempt fails because of the weather. Brings warm hat and coat for second invasion.
127 AD	**Hadrian's Wall completed** Plans drawn up for Hadrian's Shed and Swimming Pool are put on indefinite hold.
166	**First Glastonbury church is built** Rolling Stones' first festival gig in nearby field.
449	**Angles, Saxons and Jutes invade** Southern Britain quickly becomes Angleland when everyone decides to hide in a corner.

King Arthur mortally wounded
Legendary King of Britain was taken to Avalon, where his wounds were miraculously healed, according to his mediaeval chroniclers, Geoffrey of Monmouth and Richard of Wakeman.

537

Beowulf is written
Epic Anglo-Saxon poem that took 110 years to write, and was responsible for the dismissal of at least eight literary editors.

672-782

Bede completes his *History of the English*
An Anglo-Saxon who knew a deadline when he saw one, Bede completed his work at least 1,250 years ahead of schedule.

731

Danish raids start along the East coast
Alarm raised by the approaching sound of sizzling and the distinctive smell of bacon.

787

Alfred the Great becomes King of Wessex
The story of the burning cakes makes him the first of a long line of vague, unworldly monarchs.

871

Anglo-Saxon Chronicle begins
Compact edition launched later on tabloid vellum is a hit with busy, commuting tribal warmongers.

891

Alfred the Great begins building Royal Navy
Recruitment campaign fronted by the *Village People* deemed a little too advanced for its time.

893

Cnut crowned as King of England
Anglo-Saxon Chronicle is sued over minor typo-graphical error.

939

Macbeth crowned as King of the Scots
Immediately surrounded by slightly camp men who refer to him as "The Scottish King". Whistling is forbidden.

1040

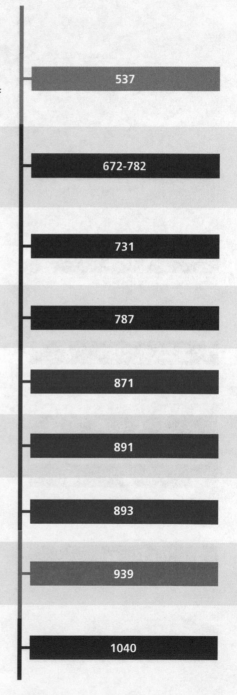

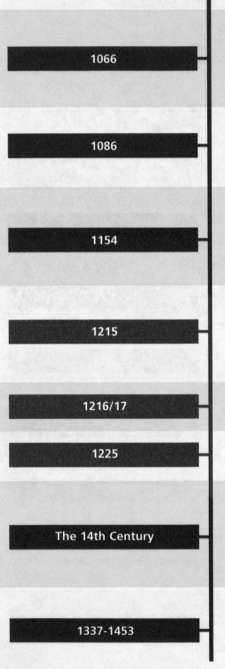

The Battle of Hastings
Normans invade, Harold II ("Eye-eye" to his friends) becomes last English King to leave his spectacles at home. William the Conqueror becomes king and invokes the ancient rite of Norman Wisdom.

1066

Domesday Book published
The concepts of doom and taxation are linked for the first time. Early adopters wait in vain for the Laser Disc edition to be released.

1086

Nicholas Breakspear becomes Pope Adrian IV
First and only English pope. Introduced Watney's Red Barrel to the Vatican and gave away Ireland to Henry II. Original inspiration for bad English behaviour abroad.

1154

Magna Carta
Very long document that sought to limit royal power, widely regarded as the first embarrassed murmurings of the British constitution, is signed by Bad King John.

1215

Magna Carta reissued twice
For signing by the new king, Henry III.

1216/17

Magna Carta reissued
With bonus content and new liner notes.

1225

Various comings and goings
Murder, machinations and general bad will prevail, every Royal escapes to France at some point, comes back, is murdered and eventually passes into legend to inspire the next generation of regal loonies. May include traces of the Black Death.

The 14th Century

Hundred Years' War declared
The fact that it would last intermittently for 116 years was cleverly concealed for the purposes of good public relations.

1337-1453

The Wars of the Roses begin
Thirty years of spasmodic butchery, this time with all-new floral branding, to settle the throne.

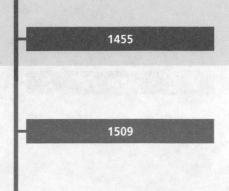

1455

Henry VIII takes throne, shortly followed by the biscuit
A badly overweight brutal man, with compulsive over-spending problems and a tendency to execute his wives. The only difference between Henry VIII and an average Oprah participant was that Henry did not live in a caravan.

1509

Magna Carta
The historic document in its entirety *(right)* and a key segment *(below)*, in which one of the meeker of the 25 barons who forced the Charter onto King John attempts to lighten what had become something of an awkward situation by adding a conciliatory "smiley" to the document. The very last paragraph, translated from the original Latin, reads "please delete as appropriate" and contains the world's first instance of an asterisk.

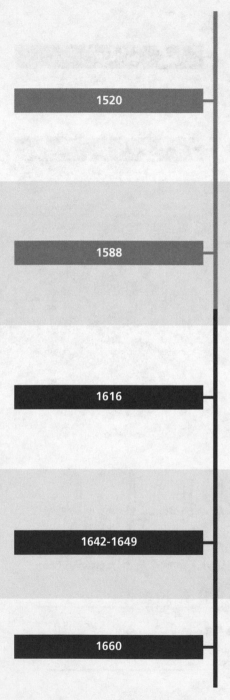

Field of the cloth of gold

Henry VIII's series of meetings with King Francis I of France were the forerunner of British diplomacy at its best. In luxurious surroundings, fountains ran with wine and each king stayed in lavishly appointed temporary palaces. The meetings were an act of goodwill, which was shattered when an alliance with the Holy Roman Empire was forged to attack France immediately after.

1520

Sir Francis Drake and the Spanish Armada

The eminent half-timbered explorer who discovered that Britain is an island and not the whole world as had been previously believed, paved the way to further discoveries of potatoes, the Spanish and cigarettes. Drake went on to rout the Spanish Armada by chasing it, Benny Hill fashion, around the coast of Britain.

1588

Shakespeare dies

In a romantic gesture gone wrong, Anne Hathaway pretends to have died. Discovering her, William is distraught and impales himself poetically on a stag's head in a melodramatic scene that lasts three hours. Tired of lying still, Anne gets up to find her husband *hath expireth of a brok'n hart*. The house then explodes.

1616

English Civil War

Parliamentarians and Royalists battled for seven years, culminating in victory for Oliver Cromwell and the beheading of Charles I. Parliament ruled for the next 11 years, but there was little in the way of democracy, except for the vote that officially made Cromwell the ugliest leader in history.

1642-1649

The Restoration

Charles II comes to the throne, which was, in the new spirit of gaiety that followed Cromwell's austere regime, fitted with whoopee cushions and golden belching funnels.

1660

The Great Plague

The last widespread epidemic of bubonic plague in these islands was responsible for the death of 70,000 Londoners, all of whom contracted it on the Northern Line, which is still coloured black on tube maps as a warning from history.

1664-1665

Act of Union with Scotland

In 1603, James IV of Scotland also became King James I of England. In the confusion of which king had what number, Shakespeare had written the prequels James II – Revenge of the Macleods and James III – The Campbells Strike Back. All this aside, it wasn't until over a hundred years later that England, Wales and Scotland were formerly unified by parliament to become Great Britain. And the rest, as they say, is British history.

1707

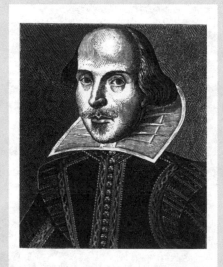

Sir William Francis Drakespeare aka Francis Bacon

The playwright and the explorer were never seen in the same room together, leading to the suspicion that they were the same man, Mr Francis Bacon, who not only wrote the plays, but circumnavigated the globe and discovered the neutrino.

Weights & Measures

Not to Scale
Lesser known units

The Yard of Ale
The bar-length dribble of beer your change is routinely dragged through before being handed to you.

Royal Mile
The mean length of travel with a member of the Royal Family from an airport in a foreign country before Britain is compromised or shamed in some way.

Stereogram
The approximate weight of a teak-effect sideboard that is half-full of Val Doonican vinyls.

For hundreds of years, Britain has measured length, width and overall thickness in units based on the dimensions of the reigning monarch and Royal Family. Founded at the height of the Empire, the measurements came to be known as Imperial. The traditional units were passed down the generations and many persist to the present day. Successive Princes of Wales, for example, have been considered important benchmarks of density.

Other units have older origins, many of which reflect an aspect of British life. For example, one British thermal unit is equal to the energy exchanged by scalding the milk in a square gross of teacups, as measured by the Scottish inventor Kilfoyle McHamilton in 1836.

On a terrace at the London Savoy, McHamilton directed cranes that manipulated an enormous fresh pot of superheated English Breakfast Tea to delicately fill a conventional porcelain cup over 20,000 times.

Before each cup was poured, an oversized creamer – mounted on a jib – dribbled milk from a height of around a hemidemisemifurlong, while 2in of jam was spread over the Strand for the sake of scale accuracy.

The experiment was judged a success when accurate measurements for the BTU were taken. McHamilton, however, became a victim of his own attention to detail, when he was crushed to death under a mile-wide paper doily at a scientific demonstration in Hove the following year.

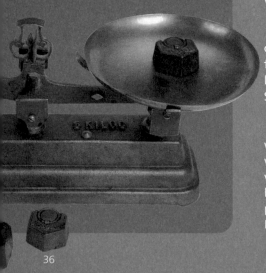

British Metric

Notwithstanding the brave and mindless dedication of scientists like McHamilton, the Imperial system was officially overturned overnight between 1970 and 1998.

No discussion about weights and measures in the UK would be complete without referring to the new values of the metric system. Fortunately, we produced a separate leaflet along those lines to save us from seeming dull in our shiny new book.

A copy of the booklet *How much do my vegetables weigh?* is freely available on presentation of a bemused questioning stare in any DoSS authorized greengrocer.

Metriconverter
Know your onions

Metric ➤ Imperial

1 g	blim
1.75g	teenth
28g	ounce
1oz	28g
16oz	1 metric pound
14lbs	1 new stone

Imperial ➤ Metric

1 fluid oz	0.65 metric sip
1pt	1 drink
8pts	1 round
1 vote	1 veto

Disclaimer

Neither the Department of Social Scrutiny, the author or the publishers of this guide can be held responsible for unforseen changes in the Weak Gravitational Force caused by quantum tunnelling, tabled amendments to the Laws of the Universe or Acts of God or UnGod. Measurements may go down as well as up.

THE
METRIC PIANO

0.15	0.25	π		%	Ctrl	Alt		Del	
C	D	E	F	G	H	J	K	L	C

Decimal music is one of the unsung benefits of metrification, and is a great showcase for the simpler life of our European "neighbours". It's easy to learn and easy to play. Whereas the eight-note English octave leaves two fingers unoccupied, the 10-note dectave has a note for every finger. What could be simpler?

It's so easy, you could master avant-garde jazz using the fingering for *Chopsticks* or play Debussy by typing a company memo. This is the fun face of metric. It's certainly more interesting than a kilogram.

We're confident that, once you hear Grieg's Base 10 Piano Concerto in H 0.75, you'll be so impressed with the metric lifestyle you'll never want to buy vegetables by the pound again.

This piano, the 10forte by Eurotinklers, is one of the new Decimal Pianos, all of which are easily identified by the words METRIC PACK stamped above middle C.

UK Emergency Services

As part of its remit to streamline public services, the Department of Social Scrutiny is to completely overhaul the way the various emergency services operate.

The Police Service
In recognition of the pivotal role that the British Bobby and Boberta play in keeping us safe, this department has answered the frequent police call for less desk work and more time on the beat. From now on, the police will complete all their paperwork out on the street, leaning against a wall.

The Fire Service
DoSS has decided to exempt the Fire Service from summertime hosepipe bans.

The Ambulance Services
The extraordinarily wasteful and ecologically unsound deployment of ambulances will stop. Paramedics and their drivers will be encouraged either to carry more than one case at a time to hospital or, where waiting for further road accidents to occur is deemed too bloodthirsty, pick up paying customers from bus stops along the way.

To cut costs and pollution further, a new scheme will be set up, utilising car parks on ring roads, where the wounded will congregate to catch an onward bus to hospital. This scheme is to be launched during early Spring next year, and will be branded as "Park 'n' Bleed".

999 Reforms

The Department of Social Scrutiny plans to further streamline the emergency services with a new and more efficient phone system.

The department has long regarded 999 as a needlessly repetitive number that can cause a gross imbalance of wear and tear to the telephone keypad. Furthermore, it is unsuited to our busy lifestyles, far too time-consuming for many and difficult to remember. For these reasons, DoSS is to change the number to a single "0". It is hoped that this change will save valuable seconds in calling out the emergency services.

We are also taking the opportunity presented by the cause of the call, to tell the caller about insurance that may be available and, where appropriate, obtain quotations for them before it is too late.

SOCIAL
SCRUTINY

Issue
THE BIRTH OF A BRITISH NATIONAL

CONTENTS

"Britain is to bees what flight is to errr, now hold on – I've got that a bit wrong."
Confused Old Man, Dyfed.

Hello Britain

Please read the following statement from the Department of Social Scrutiny to your child, once a day for a month, in a sing-song voice at bedtime. It will foster feelings of compliance and should lead to its first words being "God save the Queen".

" Welcome to the world and, specifically, Britain. We're sure that you'll enjoy your time here and grow into an essentially decent person who strives to be almost best at everything.

It's tough being a baby. There's the poo for starters. And its almost indistinguishable source – the liquidized slop on a spoon your parents pretend is an aeroplane in order to make you open your mouth in astonishment and delight, only to be disappointed once again by a mouthful of creamy chicken snot. The British sense of disillusionment in the face of authority has its roots here, but at least you have the freedom to expel a rich variety of evil-smelling by-products, each with its own distinctive aura of appallingness.

Then there are the scary spectators: people looking into your pram and scaring the living daylights out of you by squeaking at roughly the same pitch as a pipistrelle bat.

Put up with all this for a couple of years and then a competing baby comes along and your long overdue promotion to adult is completely overlooked by your parents until you are 40, bald, in charge of your own kids and just a little bitter, to be perfectly honest. Perfect material to mould the next generation of Brits. "

Britain: The Rules

You should be aware that there are some rules for being British – we'll draw your attention to these throughout the book but, broadly, they are as follows.

1   Respect your elders – they are all-knowing and wise because they have attained great age through persistence.

2   Eat your greens, but not any that involve a mining expedition up your nose.

3   It's wrong to let anything inside of you escape in public, even involuntary disembowellment and road accidents are considered unthoughtful.

4   If you use swear words on Crown property, outside the context of a discussion about art, you will be issued with vouchers for oven chips and asked to leave.

Britbaby 2005 This quintessentially British child embodies everything good about the UK. It has the brains of Alexander Fleming, the humour of an ITV sitcom writer and the physiognomy of Winston Churchill.

Great British Baby Kit

Document case with passport, ID card and false papers if caught behind enemy lines.

Cups, plates, bottles, tissues, cherry tomatoes, bibs, change of clothes (for you).

High-security, password-protected, used nappy case. Conforms to biological warfare treaties.

Case accidentally picked up last month containing details of Polaris missile programme.

Camcorder, video leads, slide projector, screen for impromptu baby photo presentations.

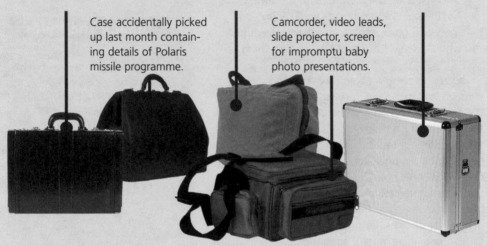

New parents easily get confused. Sleep loss, strange new liquids and the death-stirring scream of an infant can lead to lack of concentration and un-British irritability.

Which is why we have included this aide-memoire to refer to whenever you realize that you've put cat food in the potty, or you temporarily forget how to overcome a child-proof lock on a cupboard.

Above you will find identification aids to locate each item of the Sherpa mission you cheerlessly take around with baby to friends' houses, and below a simple guide to selecting the correct bottle.

NO    **NO**    **NO**    **YES**

Baby's First Jab

Why the Dodeca-Multimainline character infusion programme is the healthy choice.

What's with the needles?

1
2
3
4
5
6
7
8

Your child's injection of character-forming drugs and nano-technology is perfectly safe and has been tested on baboons, stick insects and genetically modified celery. Depending on the priorities of your local health authority, the needles may even have been washed since their last use.

1 Microscopic identity chip
2 Sense of fair play
3 Antidote to school dinners
4 Monolinguistic tendency reinforcement
5 Passive xenophobhia
6 Tartan blood dye (Celtic nations only)
7 Small pot of tea
8 Nano-bots capable of building eccentric behaviour patterns

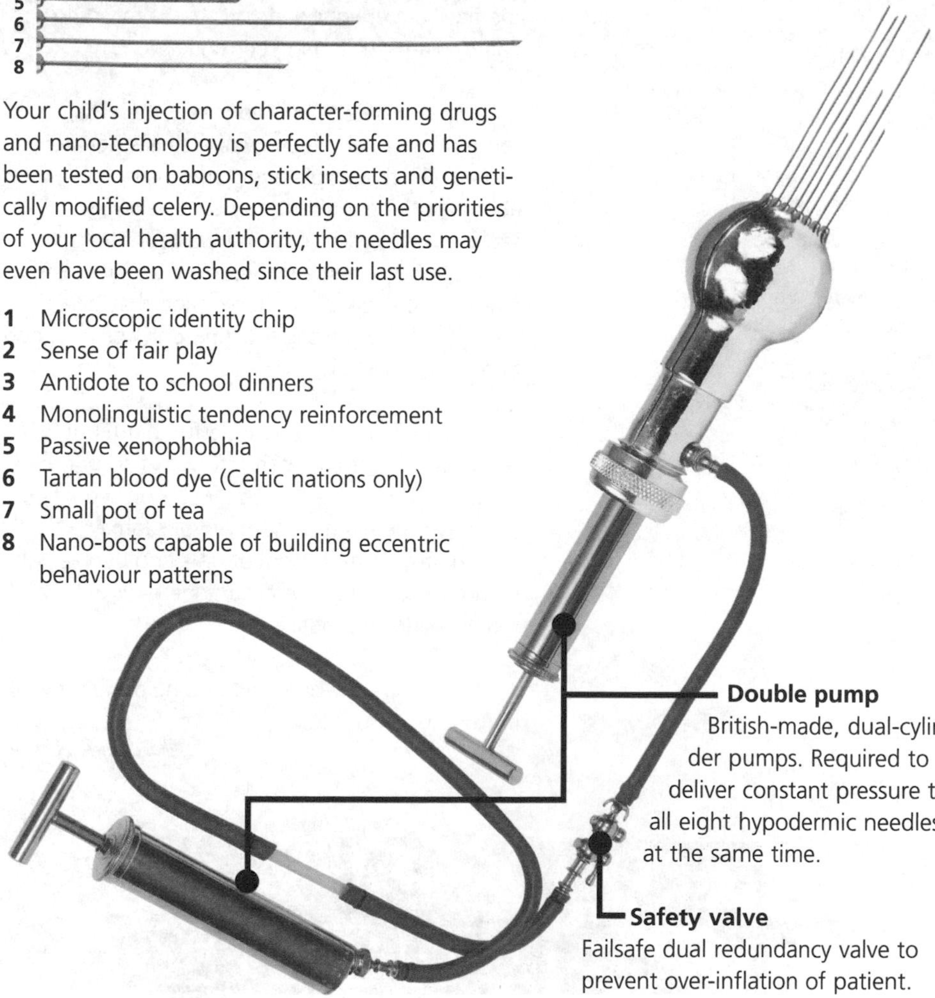

Double pump
British-made, dual-cylinder pumps. Required to deliver constant pressure to all eight hypodermic needles at the same time.

Safety valve
Failsafe dual redundancy valve to prevent over-inflation of patient.

An early start to British learning

Reading Ages

You will shortly enter a regime of continual badgering about your ability to understand writing of various levels to determine your reading age. The learning curve is very steep, and will ensure you will be able to comprehend a benefit claim form by the time you are about 75 – just after you leave college with enough letters after your name to form an entire chapter of a book on thermodynamic nuclear theory.

Being a child is magical. You look at the world through fresh eyes, and your mind is full of wonder and fascination. You may even have an imaginary friend or two – indeed, your imagination is so strong, fairy stories are as real to you as the tiger under your bed and that comforting damp, warm feeling in your underwear.

It is your parents' patriotic duty to instill a sense of national pride in you at this stage, while you are clearly gullible enough to believe just about anything without question. Taking you to see a state occasion or Royal walkabout is also critical as it will cement the idea that fairy tales really can come true. Or the notion that parliament is full of wise sages acting only for the good of all.

So imagination is a wonderful thing, but it is no substitute for cold hard facts. It is an ugly, nasty world out there as you will soon see when you leave the warm bosom of your family – or, indeed, any warm bosom at all – and people will be horrid or try to take advantage of you. It's a tough world, you hear?

Now stop your blubbing and help Mummy fill in the form opposite.

Application to send a child to school

- This form is designed with the aim of finding a place for your precious little life cargo at a state school in your area. At this stage, you should realize that all of the places at Saint Eustachian's Academy for the Fiscally Gifted were allotted before any of the actual children were conceived and, in some cases, before their parents even met.

- Places come up at other nice schools from time to time due to the occasional reluctance of potential parents to go anywhere near one another, or an informed tendency to find animals more generally trustworthy.

- Please write legibly in the spaces provided. Applications will be marked for presentation as well as comprehension.

Your child's name
You can find their name printed on a label on their shirt collar. You can save time by naming your child Gap Kid, Van Heusen or Dorothy Perkins.

How educationally advanced is your child?

☐ My child is able to solve urban traffic-flow dilemmas using only toy cars and the assistance of four Destructorbots.

☐ I'm sure the school would benefit greatly from my gift of a new library wing.

Do you consent to compulsory drug testing?

☐ The quality of my drugs is fine, thank you.

☐ They know enough about drugs already.

Is your child at all disadvantaged?

☐ It is a late developer. It has not learnt how to walk upright yet, is quite hairy, barks an abnormal amount and eats from a plate off the floor. My doctor told me it's a dog, but I have faith it isn't.

☐ Yes. I blame the parents.

Please sign the declaration.
I agree that, if accepted, my child will turn up to school every day with supplies of milk bottle tops, used bandsaw blades and other items for various pointless exercises you dream up from time to time.

Signed

In a Class of its Own

Britain's education system is the finest in the world and, for all the good intentions and fine talk about equality of opportunity, it still mercifully divides the ruling elite from the *hoi polloi*.

The Department of Social Scrutiny supports every parent's right to choose to which school they send their children, whether their background is middle-class, ruling elite or under-middle class. The following guide to education is designed to mark out the pros and cons of each establishment – weighing up the advantages of Oxbridge against the disadvantages of deprived schools.

Public school
Level: Secondary
The breeding ground of politicians, power brokers and opinion-formers, you need to send your children to a public school if they show an early interest in political thought or are precocious liars, but it will cost you. You may need to sell a folly or part of Lanarkshire to afford it, but their adult resentment of you sending them away to board will at least give you more peace in your dotage.

Old grammar school
Level: Secondary
These schools aspire to traditional principles of education that are, broadly, rigid ideas of what is good for your child, competitive sports and character-forming humiliation of 11-year-olds who have failed their entrance exams.

Inner-city comprehensive
Level: Secondary
Often a grim vision of urban decay, the inner-city "comp" is surrounded by 12-ft high chain-link fencing and authoritarian signs telling children, parents and anyone who will listen to not do

things. Children juggle flick-knives at morning break, are no longer able to spell words without the use of mobile phone numerals, and have the attention span of a concussed badger, in part due to the presence in their diet of more E numbers than the Exeter telephone directory.

Former polytechnic
Level: Higher education
These colleges – part of the 1990s boom in higher education – have tell-tale compound names like the University of Southwest Trentbanks. Architecturally, they suffer from a tendency to erect absurdly shaped annexes as some kind of modernist statement, which, like their students, face a hostile world and will never work.

Redbrick university
Level: Higher education
Formed from the 1840s on and into the early 20th century, redbrick universities embody the Victorian spirit of learning. In keeping with the values of discovery, collection and adventure which they were founded on, first-year students are required to gather and taxonomically classify entire genii of beer mats and traffic cones, and develop an interest in opiate-based relaxation techniques. Anyone displaying their ankles will be sent home to their shamed parents.

Oxbridge
Level: Higher education
Oxford and Cambridge Universities' long-held antagonism to one another dates back "absolute yonks", according to Oxford's Emeritus Professor of Pointless Rivalries, Dr Julio Inglesias. Although they try hard to welcome students from the lower classes, the heady atmosphere of the colleges would eventually corrupt the fieriest anarchist wastrel into becoming a Conservative MP with an interest in auto-erotic strangulation.

School Dinners

A handy guide to the identification of ingredients.

While most kids opt for chips and burgers for lunch, and others simply eat the nutritious plastic wrapping and labels around their subliminally cheesy snack pots, many still opt for a traditional school dinner.

This way at least, given school's proper role – that of preparing the young for certain disappointment – they deny themselves the potential for sensory pleasure as well as opportunities in the world of work.

This guide was originally part of the food section, but we realized that school dinners are more a part of the education process than the catering.

Potatoes

The Great British spud is boiled for an hour and a half to break down the cell walls, which helps to release all the goodness and flavours. Into the saucepan. It is then left to cool before serving, and is a perfect accompaniment for a meal that has no fancy ideas about flavour.

Gravy

School gravy comes in a variety of thicknesses and tastes, including a pink one which can bring on migraines and lead to higher states of consciousness but which everybody assumes is strawberry custard. All gravies have a number of things in common, however. They are all chemically inert, foldable for storage and can be lifted off the plate in one piece, without leaving a mark.

Mystery vegetable

Today's mystery vegetable was found growing by the A30. It was boiled with the French beans to remove the insouciant hints of plyboard and strychnine.

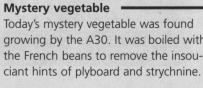

Post-traumatic French beans
After boiling with the mystery vegetable, the French beans turned this interesting colour. A colour that our vegetable cook, Linda, says she will paint the garage door as soon as she gets out of hospital.

Yorkshire pudding
The only part of the meal that is edible without prior tenderizing with a bandsaw.

Mouse
Part of a misunderstanding about *bubble and squeak*. May have recently nibbled the mystery vegetable.

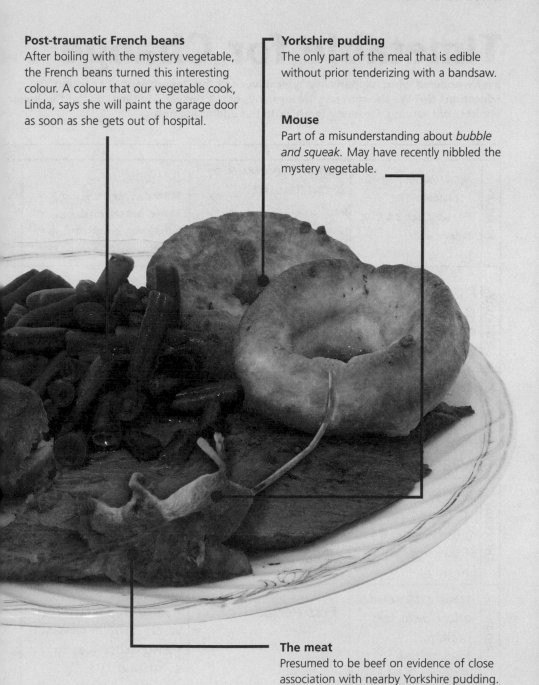

The meat
Presumed to be beef on evidence of close association with nearby Yorkshire pudding.

Timetable for Change

Ever wondered what happens in a typical week at the Department of Learning and Education? No? We thought not. Never mind, here's the weekly timetable of the Junior Minister of Learning, Dr Jenny Teeth, with her additional notes.

	1	2	3
MONDAY	Assembly @ 9. Hymn: The First Cut is the Deepest.	Report to Head of Department. My Assistant, Mr James, is such a creep - I bet he wants my job.	School Visit Remember to find some black children working on a laptop to be photographed with.
TUESDAY	Double Cabinet Meeting @ 9.30. Keep an eye on young Bladder, he seems to think he can get away with lying.		Departmental tuck shop duty.
WEDNESDAY	Rebrand Open University as Closed University in anticipation of budget cuts.	White Paper marking Remember to mention to Cabinet that 'action' is not a verb. C-	
THURSDAY	Registration. Mr James appears to be taking a lot of time off. Phone parents.	Discussion paper: "Make a child happy - close a school" Told Mr Harare he couldn't have his i-Spud back till the end of the week.	
FRIDAY	Reminder: Order additional text book for Hampshire Schools Service.	Free Period !!!	Photo opportunity with school dinner. Remember not to swallow!!!!!!

Week number . . . . 17 . . . . . . Term . . . . Spring.

You must show this sheet to your Head of Department at your weekly meeting.

4	5	6
Departmental Meeting. Caught Mr James chewing again, told him to spit it out and stand in the corner to think about what he had done.		Set homework for Juniors. Committee findings on text book acquisition and distribution.
Free Period !!!	Department Seminar: Methodology of Special Needs Learning Structures Confiscated Mr Harare's i-Spud, or whatever it's called.	
Double Home Economics Mr James seems incapable of balancing a household budget. Will put him down for remedial accountancy.		School Visit Remind security that the fat kids are not wearing belts packed with C4. We don't want an 'incident' like last Monday.
DOLE outing to the Houses of Parliament Education and Learning Questions went well, I don't think anybody noticed that I let a split infinitive slip out in all the excitement or that I counted some items of investment twice. Still, maths is not my strong point!!!		
Mr James found. Parents do not wish to talk to me for some reason?	Further Education College Visit Required to wear goggles and asked to mix chemicals together over a Bunsen burner for the cameras. I think there was an awful lot of fuss made about the explosion.	

Nibbles and Dribbles
BRITISH FOOD AND DRINK

CONTENTS

> **"A cup of tea is a medium brown mild psychotropic alkaloid."**
> DUD – The Department of Unnecessary Details.

The British National Diet

The Department of Social Scrutiny believes that Britons should always, where possible, eat and drink genuine British fare. Which is why, in line with the successful introduction of the National Curriculum for Education and the Minimum Wage for the world of work, the department is now ready to introduce the British National Diet – an approved list of typical food and drink consumed in the UK that helps make Britain the great nation that it is.

The British National Diet, or BND, will also make it easier for the government to set out its policies on nutrition, snacks, liquid refreshment and related prandial affairs. It is hoped that the diet will re-establish the traditional British meal to the position it occupied before exotic foods like whole pineapples and other non-tinned produce were introduced.

Broadly speaking, the British National Diet aims to encapsulate just what it is that makes British cooking the art that it is. Boiling, deep-frying and roasting take precedence over subversive, foreign concepts such as "Mediterranean cuisine" and "flavour".

To find out more, come to BOILCON, the BND event at the National Propaganda Centre in spring. Turn to page 64 for more details.

British tea Beloved of toothless East End hags, smart city slickers and chinless nobs alike, the cuppa will shortly become a Class D drug, since a recent spate of thefts was blamed on addicts funding their habit.

Food on the Go

Take-aways

Approximately 12 hours after they have nibbled through low-fat, high-fibre lunches, many Britons can be found roaming the streets drunk, looking for some of the following take-aways.

Fish and chips (*above*)
The great British deep-fried festival of lard served with a pot of pale green bicycle paint affectionately known as "mushy peas".

Kebab
Carved from a spit-roasted 80lb slab of God-knows-what, merely holding a kebab confirms you have finally exhausted all your powers of reason.

Chicken in a bucket
Following consumption, this early-hours favourite does at least provide a convenient receptacle (*right*) for refilling by means of an anti-peristaltic reflex.

A quick bite "on the hoof" can take a number of forms in Britain from gazelle-like nibbling of an unlikely sounding sandwich at lunchtime to a full-blown after-pub gut-buster (*left*).

A light lunch usually means a cold meat pie, pasty or sandwich wrapped in cellophane with a card insert that details its various nutritional qualities, while rustic prose about cows that have not been fed on other cows effortlessly rambles on about how all the ingredients come from places with poetic-sounding names. Most Britons make do with fairly plain fare, but upmarket female consumers are often tempted by more exotic "wraps" because they colour co-ordinate with their pashminas.

Every effort is made to convince the consumer that the food is healthy, despite the fact it must be inhaled during a 10-minute lunch break, avoiding the manic pink-eyed gaze of a mutant pigeon with one and a half legs in a small park thick with the slightly sweet smell of dog faeces.

Below: Gazelle-like nibbling.

relax, have a cup of tea

*H*ard day on the tube? Bad afternoon at the office? Tired of the Machiavellian scheming and mendacious, twisted dishonesty of the puppet state?

Hey! Don't bust a blood vessel, man. You need to chill out. You don't need a *coup d'état,* you need a cup of tea.*

Whether it's a family crisis, a medical emergency, a government scandal or an international "situation" involving massive loss of life in pursuit of control of the oil industry, a cup of tea will soon sort everything out.

When the counter-reactionary backlash starts, the Blitz Spirit just won't be complete without gallons of hot tea and the ceremonial minutiae of warming the pot, scalding the milk and passing the biscuits. Anthrax on the overground? Ricin in the food chain? Unspecified toxic compounds in your water supply? No matter, just pop the kettle on and everything will be OK.

Remember: the French drink coffee and they had a revolution. There's no need for that here.

The following pages contain full details of how to respond to an emergency using a tea-based methodology.

* *Please phone the MI5 Terrorism Helpline if you are planning a coup.*

Notes on drinking tea

Please Read Carefully

These notes contain important information regarding the serving of beverages at higher than ambient room temperature for the purposes of, but not limited to: thirst satiation; amelioration or partial satisfaction of cravings for mild, psychotropic alkaloids; oral pleasure; or the commission of a ritualistic act of social cohesion, such as a tea break or a scheduled mid-afternoon liaison with a Minister of the Church of England, otherwise known as a vicar.

This leaflet should not be considered a full and authoritative statement of etiquette, and applies only to mid-range teas between Earl Grey and English Breakfast. Lapsang Souchong drinkers are advised to soak this leaflet in pine disinfectant, obtain an acetate copy and project it onto the side of an albino French poodle in order to mirror their hollow lifestyle of pointless sensation and effect.

Now continue on next page

Tea Gauge
How does your brew measure up?

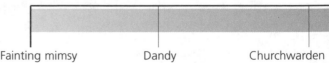

Fainting mimsy   Dandy   Churchwarden

734-71M3

Selection of crockery determines social position. A mug may be used either within 18ft of an open manhole or within a warehouse environment – namely within 39in of either a stepladder or a volume of cardboard greater than a quarter of a cubic yard. For all other purposes, a cup and saucer are the only option.

The host/ess is responsible for the distribution of tea, and indicates commencement of pouring with an assumptive phrase like "Shall I be mother?" after an awkward silence of greater than 2.9 seconds stemming from a lapse in conversation or an unforeseen rectal interjection from an elderly relative.

Milk should be added before the tea is poured, for reasons of complex thermodynamics as well as strict government flood prevention guidelines.

You should leave a little tea in the cup for the purposes of fortune telling, or for warding off the lascivious attentions of members of the opposite sex aroused by the heady combination of lace doillies and the overt fingering of sponge.

Now stop reading ●

Warning
Very hot tea may be hot and, in some cases, very hot.

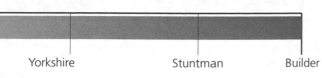

Yorkshire   Stuntman   Builder

Notes on cake and miscellaneous confectionery

Please Read Carefully

Accompanying your tea with cake or miscellaneous confectionery is your patriotic, legal duty, unless you are the subject of a Crumb Restraint Order. In which case, you are entitled to disregard these pages, provided you maintain a distance of not less than 100yds between you and all items of confectionery.

These notes concern the serving, presentation and subsequent consumption of light sponge, cake, scones and/or other items defined as confectionery beyond reasonable doubt by a qualified Doctor of Patisserie, or a quorum of a competent academic panel overseeing a qualifying postgraduate study of biscuits. Except where exclusions or exceptions by law apply, pudding is not allowed.

Different rules apply to savoury snacks. If you are in receipt of savoury snacks, you must tell us at once, or your cup of tea may be delayed, suspended or withdrawn altogether. If you have already received your tea, you may be asked to return it to us in the envelope provided. If you are not sure whether your snack is savoury, tell us anyway and we will work it out for you.

Now look at the picture

Teatime glossary

Tea *(n)* **1.** An all-purpose drink served on an *ad hoc* basis throughout the day to enable targets of social cohesion and refreshment to be met. **2.** *(informal, Northern, wrong)* An evening meal analogous to *dinner* south of Spalding. *Usage example: "Oscar made himself a nice pot of* **tea** *and gaily shot the first trespasser of the day from his verandah."*

734-c4k3

Now read on ↓

The rules regarding whether to use fingers or a cake fork during confectionery consumption are very complex, and will depend on a case-by-case basis. Broadly speaking – though it is not an authoritative statement of the law – cakes require a fork and biscuits may be manoeuvred by hand, but the status of pastries depends on overall flakiness and the outcome of a case currently before the European Court of Human Rights.

Biscuits may be manipulated by the thumb and forefinger for the purposes of executing a brief immersion, otherwise known as "dunking". It is important, however, during the immersion process, to hold the little finger aloft, as if you were handling a bag of turds, in order to foster an atmosphere of gentle dignity.

If you wish to receive further information about tea-time confectionery, you should seek advice from a chartered charlady or see the Department of Social Scrutiny's leaflet, "What is a Biscuit?", available at all DoSS offices, taped to the hind quarters of a hungry, barking Alsatian.

Now stop reading ●

High tea *(n)* **1.** An evening meal, of a substantial manner, at which tea, the drink, is served.
Usage example: "Miriam regretted that Oscar couldn't come to **high tea** *because she had carefully planned the placement of biscuits, and had nervously fingered her paper doillies all afternoon."*

BOILC⊙N ⁰⁶

The Department of Social Scrutiny is proud to present the first annual event to celebrate the new British National Diet. BOILCON draws together the food industry, politicians, food regulators and MI5 under the same roof to eat, drink and mount surveillance operations on anyone daring to ask for couscous during the event.

This first year, we are concentrating on the introduction of the British National Diet – a bold new policy to manage the nutritional needs of the nation in a consistent manner. Restaurants and supermarkets will be required to mark prepared meals with the National Diet Charter Mark. To help consumers make sense of the scheme, the folowing classifications will be used.

BND Key Stage 1 – Starters
BND Key Stage 2 – Main course
BND Key Stage 3 – Pudding or dessert
BND Key Stage 4 – Cheese and/or mint-
infused chocolate wafers

Other Key Stages will be approved, depending on how hungry civil servants working on the classification scheme become.

Finally, the Department of Social Scrutiny would like to thank all delegates for attending the first ever BOILCON. Thanks to your efforts – and the application of a certain amount of oppression – British food like over-boiled vegetables and cauterized meat will once again take its rightful place at the head of the menu.

A Department of Social Scrutiny exhibition about British food

Exhibition Facts

Where is it?
BOILCON '06 takes place at the National Propaganda Centre, located on the banks of Birmingham's famous Alimentary Canal.

What is there?
Stalls, displays and seminars (see *right*) about British food and the new National Diet.

The exhibition is arranged like the human gut tract. You enter, via the Mouth, into the Oral Mastication Room. Darkened and slightly moist, this display is dedicated to getting you to chew your food properly, and you will be held here for 10 minutes before joining the Peristaltic Escalator to the rest of the exhibition.

After time spent in the Oesophagus Corridor and the Stomach Room, your journey through the Intestine Complex can be broken with a stop-off at the Appendix Café – a temporary room that may be removed at any time.

After several hours, the urge to leave will be unavoidable. An exit through the Rectal Atrium and on to a waiting bus to Digbeth coach station will complete your journey from dinner plate to toilet. We hope you enjoyed your visit to BOILCON '06, and look forward to seeing you over the years to come.

Fish and Chips and the Post-Structuralist Discourse on Re-contextualized Food Memes
Tartare sauce has been found culturally void. Please bring your own vinegar.
Sponsored by the Troubled Sole Psychiatric Chip Shop.

Yorkshire Pudding: Re-integrating the Hermeneutic Perspective
Yorkshire pudding is mentioned only nine times in the Bible. What can be done about this?

Deconstructing Lard
What is it that lard is trying to say, exactly?

Roast Beef: Towards a Self-Reflexive Understanding of Gravy
Britain's Sunday favourite is served within a medium constructed from the meal itself – meat and vegetable stock radicalized by a thickening agent. What does this say about the role of gravy as both content and container?

Further seminars in brief

Cauliflower Cheese in the Age of Enlightenment

Reflections on the Consensus Reality of the Potato

Understanding Broccoli

Convenience Food

Busy career? Not enough time on your hands to cook for you or your family? It's not hard to see why the national diet includes such a generous helping of convenience food.

Food on Your Lap

Type of food
Virtually instant convenience food manufactured from God-knows-what in a giant shed with no natural lighting in the vicinity of Birmingham.

Presentation
Bright and breezy packaging that holds some clues as to what all the pre-teenage children's comic designers are up to these days. Often features a friendly stereotypical animal character tastefully unrelated to the animal in the packet.

Adult versions of these meals are packaged in a subtler way, with lots of nice cursive lettering and panels printed in gold ink.

Sold principally to single, carefree, career-focussed individuals, packaging is designed to forestall any sense of disappointment right up to the moment that you consume it, heartbroken and alone, at your kitchen table.

Britons work the longest hours of any employees in Europe, and that's something the Department of Social Scrutiny is tremendously proud of.

The only fly in the tub of soothing ointment we apply daily to the weeping sore of indolence, is the sometimes difficult matter of finding enough time to eat. Which is where convenience food comes in – simple to cook, quick to prepare, and very easy to eat, there's no need to miss a moment of work ever again.

British convenience food comes in several varieties, from replica motorway service area meals to elaborate creamy pasta dishes that can either be eaten hot from a microwave or applied cold as a moisturiser.

The most important facet of convenience food is that it should be presented in a way that excites the busy diner. According to a recent study, saliva is good for you again, and modern foods take this into account with serving suggestions designed to make you salivate wildly on eye contact with the packaging.

Cap'n Hermaphrodite's Fishish Fingers *(right)* is a typical packet of convenience food aimed at the family market. It features bright, primary colours, an encouraging photograph to elicit the production of saliva, along with the added value of a slightly disturbing caricature that somehow communicates with the dark recesses of your child's mind.

Rich in lady-enhancing hormones & tidal slurry
FISHY BUSINESS
Trawling the depths for you!
Cap'n Hermaphrodite's
Fishish Fingers
Arr, ma hearties!!! my fingers are extra fishy today!!
Serving suggestion only
Indication of a Mediterranean lifestyle and a certain careless generosity with herbs is no guarantee that said lifestyle and herbs are enclosed within.

Ingredients

Mechanically recovered animal protein (fish lips, arseholes, ground fins, optic nerve tissue), genetically modified tidal slurry, ground crab brain, sweepings.

Allergy/Legal Advice

We're not entirely sure but this product may contain fish, nuts, fingernails and the odd Reed Warbler or two. Please don't sue us.

Special Diets

This product is suitable for lacto-pisco-vegetarians who also eat beef and secretly murder horses.

This product is suitable for sado-masochists.

Safety Advice

Please tell your doctor immediately if you suffer from any or all of the following after you consume this product: Itchy tongue, feelings of paranoia, renal failure, burning, enlarged eyes, swelling of face, death.

Nutrition

100g contains 800% of your RDA for cadmium, organo-phosphates, oestrogen and pseudopopsiphetamine-dichloride.

Storage Advice

Once opened, consume immediately inside fume cupboard. Do not freeze, refreeze, defrost, refrigerate or store.

Packaged in a defective atmosphere.

Environmental Information

Product:
80% post-consumer waste.

Packaging:
Steel, plastic, glass, paper, carbon-fibre. Recyclable, where facilities exist. Which they don't.

Preparation

To microwave.
Pierce film lid and text COOK, followed by the barcode to the number on inner pack. Place phone in dish, with antenna in food. After 2nd Peter Andre ringtone, remove phone and arrange food diagonally on plate and away from body, in order to minimize radio interference and potential spontaneous human combustion.

Cap'n Hermaphrodite's Fishish Fingers With its easy to understand instructions and option of phone radiation cooking, this meal offers fantastic convenience with only a medium to high increased risk of immediate death.

What is in a Burger?

You may well ask, but chances are you don't want to know the answer.

And neither did the Ministry of Nutrition, but it sent one off for lab testing and found out anyway. This is its report.

Foliage

Lettuce grown to be indistinguishable from the flavour and texture of poly-thene, so as not to detract from the heavily enhanced burger in any way. Available in super-limp and corrugated tutu versions.

The bap

Specially formulated roll with enough yeast to nurture life all over again in the event of an ecological melt-down. Also available with small plastic studs that mimic the effect of sesame seeds.

Burger

Homogenized slip-cast beef slurry burger with flavour enhancers. Features geneti-cally modified cow hormones that, when ingested over time, will lead you to develop a hopeless illogical fascination with five-bar gates.

Epoxy Cheese

Specially developed for NASA, this heat-proof cheese is diecast to key into the burger in any of four orientations, and is styled as pseudo-melted. The top surface features an indentation tray that will accommodate a slice of size 7 tomato.

Tip: To find out what healthstyle options are available to counter fast food, turn the page.

98%
food free

Snacks are great, aren't they?

They help you to live the life you live the life of, without breaking for one moment longer than it takes to nosebag a few grams of enhanced sawdust down your needy gape.

But the problem with ordinary snacks is that they all contain one element that scientists** agree will eventually kill you. It's not just fat, sugar and salt you should be worried about. Every snack you eat contains food.

Food wears down your gut and erases you from the inside out. Until now, that is.

BowelBunga Liteplus is the new 98% food-free polyethylene biscuit you need to get you through your day of dizzying deadlines and remorseless, brain-buggering tedium. Every BowelBunga contains enough appetite suppressant to keep you from the fridge for a day, while pioneering* biscuit brush technology will ensure no scrap of food will linger in your gut long enough to add a potentially disfiguring calorie.***

BowelBunga Liteplus. Go on, starve yourself.

 *   Does not contain pies.
 ** This reference was removed in order to deliberately
      promote a sense of mystery and intrigue.
*** Removal of BowelBunga will require a corkscrew, a
      willing friend, 10 Newtons of force and a clean towel.

Farmer Suticle Foods

Healthy Eating

The government, through its Ministry of Nutrition, has noticed that the rate of rise in the increase of speed of the trend of growth in fast-food consumption is now beginning to level out. So, you may well ask, what does this actually mean?

It means that while we cannot be complacent about the figures, we are winning the battle against the fight mounted against the argument that we need to stop. While recognizing the strains placed on hard-working families, we would urge you to be uncomplacent.

There are a number of ways to combat the trends. First of all, you could simply eat less fast food – but this is probably too radical a solution for most families who rely, to some extent, on releasing a tide of subtly addictive flavours and mind-altering cattle hormones into their children to get some peace and quiet.

An alternative to radical measures like eating less has emerged with a new wave of medical non-foods. Styled using consensus notions of what constitutes "delicious", medical non-foods contain almost no nutritional value whatsoever, yet satisfy your appetite and craving as if they did. The BowelBunga range of quasi-biscuits was one of the first non-food products to come to market and its success was instant. The next product to be launched is expected to be the Polypizzylene, an inert, spongey dough with epoxy cheese and a false tomato on top.

Vegetarianism

You may have heard of this – but don't be put off by the fact that most vegetarians look unhealthy and exhibit poor taste in popular music. There are routes to becoming vegetarian, without giving up meat. Here are a few suggestions.

1 Become a piscovegetarian. These vegetarians eat fish because they have examined their consciences, and believe that fish are hopelessly stupid and deserve to die.

2 Eat only white meat. The argument is extended to encompass other intellectually inferior animals, such as the chicken.

3 Become a vegetarian-once-removed and stop consuming animals that in turn eat other animals. This is handy because it passes the moral dilemma down the food chain one step, and allows you to eat cows.

 Virtually food-free-food Products like BowelBunga radically alter attitudes to food. There was a three-fold increase in purchases of corkscrews after a recent BowelBunga television advertising campaign.

Another method is to eat to excess those foods that are good for you, in the same way that you eat too many unhealthy things. Healthy food contains vitamins, minerals and roughage, as well as guilt-relieving properties that directly balance-out bad food. And the worse it tastes or the more unfortunate the texture, the greater the value to you. A typical tactic would be to eat a whole raw cabbage in order to eat a pound of Belgian chocolate.

The process of compensation applies to the circumstances and manner of consumption as much as the taste. Lunch taken at your desk, for example, contains less harmful guilt than even the healthiest sandwich taken at leisure in the park.

The Ministry of Nutrition is now trying to send these kinds of messages to the British people, so that we can win the battle against the fight mounted against the argument that we all need to stop and eat safely. Having said that, Britain is still a much safer place to eat than some parts of Europe. France, for example, has an astonishing knack of consuming meals prepared from garden pests, while Italy regards a sparrow as a delicacy. Remember that the next time you order pizza.

Called to the Bar

British drinks, a Department of Social Scrutiny review

Britons have a special aptitude for being drunk and are rightly famous the world over for it. Whether it's lager-fuelled football hooligans or Scotch-doused MPs, getting inebriated is a national pastime and is as much a part of our heritage as over-boiled vegetables, tea and losing at sport.

So it is fitting that, in this book about Britain, the Department of Social Scrutiny should relax a little – in strict accordance with official guidelines – and spend a little time sampling the delights of the local British hostelry.

Over the next three pages, we detail the drinks that can be commonly found in British bars, and then focus on the institution that is the public house itself.

Not to scale

Real ale

Working class gut-filler served from a diseased medieval pump at room temperature. A real ale drinker can grow a respectable beard in a day, but many do not stop there and go on to develop an unhealthy interest in folk music, computer programming or Celtic languages.

Lager

Principally consumed by louts and other people who believe they have a sense of humour, lager has become steadily stronger over the years. Some of the more exotic brands can now be used to fuel light aircraft, or be mixed with cider to make excellent cleaning fluid.

Alcopops

Fizzy, sweetened compound of spirit and mixer, popular among feral children and their nominally adult counterparts. A similar drinking experience to lemonade, but instead of a brief sugar buzz before you kiss your parents goodnight, you may unaccountably find yourself in a hotwired Fiesta, being chased up the M40 by a convoy of swerving police cars.

Wine

Nothing underlines the British attitude to drinking better than wine. The French regard it merely as liquid food, to be savoured as part of a meal, while the British pub has largely turned its consumption into an exercise in getting gently, but industrially, pissed – a process attacked with characteristic British vigour and determination.

Cocktail

Something of an alcoholic pick 'n' mix, drinking cocktails is essentially just serious drinking dressed up with accessories. Slices of fruit, olives, ice and the odd miniature parasol will not mitigate the brain-blowing fusion of tipples you have assembled your drink from. Generally, the more flamboyant the cocktail, the more you should be wary of the drinker.

Cider

Cider drinkers lean on country gates giving bad directions to lost motorists as part of a rural conspiracy to re-mystify the countryside. A stronger variant, farmhouse scrumpy, has an even more pronounced effect, and is implicated in the creation of a race of super-strength, straw-sucking psychopaths that dance naked through the night at unmanned stone circles.

Gin

A catastrophic addiction in the offing, gin attracts drinkers from both the slow sip and the intravenous ends of the market. Its present use as a suburban muscle-relaxant is laudable, but you can relive its dark past – it was the ruin of 18th-century London – with supermarket gin, a bottle of which is marginally more challenging than barbecue fluid.

Scotch

Scotch drinkers would like you to think that, in drinking terms, they are gentlemen among thieves. Their vocabulary of wafty adjectives ranks as frankly silly, particularly when you consider that chilled creosote has roughly the same effect as the ludicrously priced piss-pot full of ethanol that apparently has a "smokey burn". Steer clear.

Tequila

In most formulations, tequila is a drink that has elevated getting drunk to a bitter and warped fetish. After a few slammers, drinkers typically develop a glazed, maniacal stare that could cut through zinc, and many will actually try. A quick and dirty brain-steamer that is not at all British, but is included here as a warning to you all.

Absinthe

Considered something of a radical tipple, if you're looking for a different kind of drink, absinthe will fit the bill. Or you could try electric convulsive therapy, which has the same effect, but will not stain your tie. If you find an empty absinthe bottle on a bar, it's possible the user is beyond their most effective in terms of thwarting their inherent lunacies.

A Guide to the British Drinking Establishment

Swinging open the doors of an assortment of hostelries, the Department of Social Scrutiny looks for the perfect British public house.

The Department of Social Scrutiny takes the view that the British pub is a unique place of refuge in a busy world, but it has come to our attention that this quintessentially British institution could be in danger of dying out.

Where once our streets were lined with honest British public houses, our towns and cities are now dominated by bars where drinkers are forced to relax in some kind of themed environment. This has now gone so far that, in one recent case, a traditional pub in Lancaster was stripped bare of all its furnishings and fixtures and re-opened several weeks later themed as itself, having been re-named "The Olde Needless Reiteration".

It will come as no surprise, then, that theme pubs with quirky names like "The Spigot and Nostril" or "The Famous Celeriac" have spread like wildfire, effectively engulfing the licensed habitat. What is surprising, perhaps, is that there is still plenty of choice.

On a more sober note, the department has long felt that a solution to binge drinking is necessary, and can recommend a number of soluble tablets for this very purpose. However, we have

Left: "The Diptheria Arms". A forgotten corner of the balance sheet.

❝ Frequented by Ted Heath lookalikes, this inn oozes with the braying twittery of the wealthy classes. ❞

come to the conclusion that prevention is better than cure, and that British drinkers drink excessively because the current licensing laws do not give them enough time to drink sensibly.

After a broad and wide-ranging consultation in many, many public houses, we are now seeking to avoid the spectacle of massed gangs of yobs roaming the streets causing trouble at closing time, by simply outlawing closing time.

In sampling the hospitality of the fine hostelries over the next few pages, we trust you'll eventually see the sense of this move.

"The Poor Anchors"

Located on the harbourside of a south-coast, nautically minded town, and frequented by Ted Heath lookalikes, amiable buffoons and overspill from the local yacht club, this inn oozes the braying twittery of the wealthy classes.

A yachty inn is a very loud place. More used to issuing commands in the teeth of gales, nautical types approach bars with the gravitas of a cruise liner in a duck pond. With bar staff rendered utterly deaf by their overbearing customers, the easiest way to order a pint is to let off distress flares at the door and signal with flags.

Pub Games

Pub darts

Athletes stand on a line – the Hockey – exactly 9ft from a soft, round board screwed to a wall at a height of 68in, and drink beer until they are no longer capable of hitting it with a sharpened metal dart.

Pool

A game of skill that involves hitting a ball with another ball that is, in turn, propelled with great force by a long stick down a cloth-covered table. The aim is to propel the balls all over the table, the pub and, eventually, through the pub window by the artful use of brute force.

"The Dead Badger"

Usually found in a remote moorland village with a somewhat dried-up gene pool, the first time you walk into this village pub there is a brief and slightly disconcerting silence as all the shotguns are partly concealed, and a deputation from the snug is sent to search police photofits for your likeness.

Once the formalities are over, however, it's straight down to the old country pub customs of telling ghost stories, wassailing and cheating at dominoes while a local lynch mob gathers outside in the shadows of the unlit car park.

"The Diptheria Arms"

A traditional brewery-owned house, located in a hard-to-find back-street of a large city, this pub does not exist in a financial sense at all, after a rash of brewery mergers and acquisitions misplaced it somewhere along the way. Personal tankards line the shelves, and a man who has not been home for three years perches at the bar flirting with the staff in a way that only a seasoned drunk can manage.

"Ye Olde Motel"

Found in town centres, on ring roads and absolutely everywhere else.

Despite its name, a modern pub that in its misguided stab at antique charm looks as if it was flooded with mahogany wood stain at some point in its brief history. All the furniture is so clean and reflective, you could be forgiven for thinking that you were drinking in a kaleidoscope.

Pub Games

Dominoes
An important indicator of how far you are actually prepared to go to amuse yourself, a game of dominoes reduces the pub experience to a tiresome night with people with whom you have absolutely nothing in common. Preceded by a conversation about soap operas, and culminating in a vicious argument about your loveless marriage.

"The Famous Smackhouse"

Found near a large and threatening high-rise estate, this inner-city pub is famed for its drive-by shootings and the police surveillance team parked in an unmarked Mondeo across the road.

Your host for the evening is a man called Skull who has only three fingers on one hand and your throat in the other. The knife scar on his cheek is so extensive it contains knife scars of its own.

"The Inebriated Salesman"

Incorporating conference rooms and other business facilities, these chain-hotels are often developed around an existing pub that happens to be located close to a motorway junction or airport.

Similar in atmosphere to "Ye Olde Motel", in that it has none, the bar features a carpet of unparalleled depth and softness and a variety of beers that are identical, whichever taps they happen to come from. Often full of pissed company reps on inter-personal skills courses, letting their hair, as well as their spouses, down.

"The Mao Se Tun"

Located in a trendy part of a major cosmopolitan city, this wine bar is a chi-chi minimalist enclave where the furniture and clientele are arranged according to the principles of feng shui, the Chinese science of storage solutions.

Right: "Ye Olde Motel". Flooded with mahogany wood stain.

SOCIAL SCRUTINY

First Steps

TRAVEL AND TRANSPORT

CONTENTS

"Even a journey of a thousand miles begins with a single to Wrexham."
Brecknock and Radnorshire aphorism

Getting Around Britain

Despite long traditions of trackways and roads for thousands of years before the Romans, Britain's transport infrastructure didn't become formalized until the mid-19th century. Now under the aegis of the Department of Motion (DoMo), the British transport network includes over five and a half billion cubic yards of premium airspace, and 40,000 miles of rail track arranged as matched pairs in negative redundancy arrays. This works out at 20,000 miles of actual railway.

The department is responsible for the regulatory framework for the railways. For all inquiries regarding codes of practice and rail regulatory external grievance nodes, contact the Rail Tsar at:

OffRails
Mr Frederick Puffy McSteam Gasket
The Old Railway Station
Signalpost
Deepest Berkshire

If you are just looking for details of your nearest Users' Committee, DoMo would like to thank you for your interest whilst regretfully informing you that participants in all Users' Committees are chosen entirely at random from a sample of horse-faced commuters that DoMo officials follow home from the station, and kidnap in the dead of night to avoid opinion contamination. However, thank you for your interest in our representative democracy. Have a nice journey.

DoMo

The Department of Motion is without a fixed office and travels the length of Britain, discharging its responsibilities to road, rail and leg users alike.

In order to be seen to be free from any kind of mainstream vehicular bias, DoMo moves about the country by roving narrowboat. Employees are the only public sector workers compelled to wear lifebelts at their desks. As part of a risk-conscious, regulatory-intense health and safety node, DoMo desks have now also been fitted with airbags.

Below: DoMo boats meet for a regional conference.

One of the DoMo's new pelican crossing designs for the increasingly dangerous 21st century. Other models feature warnings for dirty bombs, asylum seekers and radioactive killer frogs free-falling from the sky.

Going the Right Way

New Roads

DoMo has recently embarked on a massive programme of 21st-century road improvements. Here are some of the highlights.

- M3/M25 disentanglement.

- New ford crossing for Thames Estuary at Thurrock.

- Movement of M8 6yds to the south.

- Traffic calming measures on A1, including the erection of random brick walls across the carriageways.

- Installation of new mini roundabouts on popular long-distance footpaths to help eliminate congestion.

- Removal of Milton Keynes from Primary Route Network because of failure to meet style criteria.

- Movement of M8 7yds to the north.

- Upgrade Silverstone with yellow box junctions and Park and Ride facilities.

DoMo is responsible for more than a quarter of a million miles of roads in Britain – which would be enough to get to the moon, though it should be made clear that DoMo contractors have statutory duties to maintain the road network only as far as Aberdeen or, on Sundays, Watford.

The roads that DoMo do maintain come in four flavours, and are classified and numbered according to their usefulness from motorways (M), through primary A and junior A roads, to secondary B roads.

Britain's most important and useful road is the M1 – the London to Yorkshire motorway – and the most useless is the B9998, which is a little shorter than this book and is only maintained to safeguard the numerological coherence of the classification system, and replaces the B9999, which was wiped out by the installation of a fire hydrant cover last year. Road numbering became briefly prominent during the 1970s when there was a fashion for naming major crimes after them, as well as a selection of international standard paper sizes.

These days, road numbers are chiefly used by people, usually men, who have just arrived at a party. To fill awkward conversational gaps upon the guest's arrival, the host may enquire of the other as to the route taken, which will lead to a good-natured, yet pointed, debate featuring a road atlas. Guests who do not eventually see the sense of the incumbent male's proposed route may be treated with disdain.

Rites of Way

Modern motorists need only to remind themselves to mirror, signal and manoeuvre in order to remember the exact course of action when approaching a junction, but it was not always so easy for our ancestors.

At the turn of the 20th century, as illustrated in the case study to the right, if more than one gentleman driver was on the same carriageway, they had to establish who had right of way by a complex calculation involving class status and exact position relative to the throne. The more aristocratic driver was allowed to drive much as he pleased, swerving and careering all over the road if he so wished – a custom that is still very much alive today.

At road junctions, the status of the carriageway as a whole – as defined by the gentlemen drivers upon it – was taken into account in order to determine the exact rights of way. The mathematical calculation involved in the exact etiquette of complex junctions could take hours to determine. At such occasions, evening dinner would be served on the junction until rights of way could be confirmed. The clockwise passage of the various serving staff and butlers around the table is the forerunner of the modern roundabout.

Apex Corner Case Study

As complex road etiquette calculations are worked out in 1905 (*above*), a satisfying meal of lightly grilled red deer with elm leaf salad is served, leading to an agreeably planned junction, with orderly traffic flow for many years to come.

The 20th century saw the concept of etiquette, as a means of determining right of way, diminish, with what Lord Axlebridge of Shudder presciently termed "The Ghastly Traffic Lantern", as long ago as 1976 (*right*).

"I implore every right-thinking driver to ignore them," said Axlebridge, shortly before he was arrested for conspiracy to pervert the course of traffic.

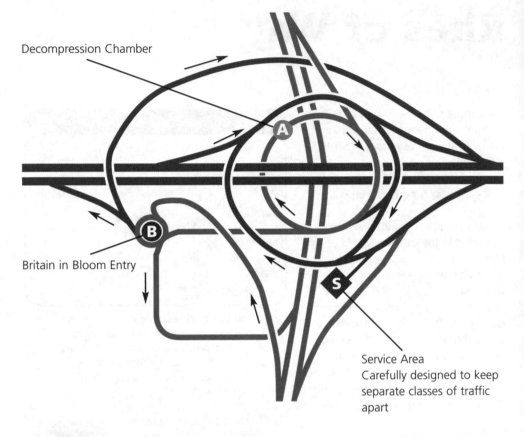

Decompression Chamber

A

Britain in Bloom Entry

B

S

Service Area
Carefully designed to keep
separate classes of traffic
apart

Anatomy of a Motorway Junction

This is Britain's most advanced motorway junction, popularly known as the "Eye of God", but known formally as junction 4B of the M654, near North Pleurisy-in-Earnest.

It is a Class V, partially graded super interchange, also known as a Vortex-plan junction. Not only is it designed to be per-

fect in every detail, but also completely dynamic in design. Traffic scientists can instantly change direction of traffic flow by the movement of just three barriers, and eight family saloon insurance write-offs. This will be particularly useful in heightened contraflow situations, such as the reversal of the Earth's magnetic poles.

The Road Ahead

Modern British motorway junctions like the "Eye of God" (*left*) incorporate many new technologies to enrich and simplify the total junction experience for drivers.

For example, motorists can subscribe to interesting daily emails chock-full of fun facts and trivia about their favourite graded interchanges, or get junction-specific horoscopes on RDS or DAB-enabled radios. And now, in the event of minor lapses of driver judgment, motorists can even be conveniently cautioned and arrested by text message (*below*).

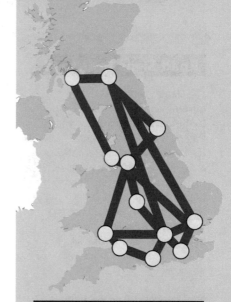

Further innovations in the world of roads and transport include an ingenious GPS in-car navigation system that delivers on its promise to get you to your destination by helping to locate your road atlas. But the most exciting development in the pipeline is travel via personal missile, where driver and passenger are delivered as a warhead to the endpoint of their destination. This system has already been successfully tested with mice "just for a laugh".

U DO NOT HAV 2 SAY NE THING BT IT MAY HRM UR DFENS IF U DO NOT MENTN WEN QSTND SMTHNG WCH U L8R RLY ON IN CRT

Curing Air Congestion

Growing demand for air travel could quickly fill all of the UK's half a billion cubic yards of air space, but the Department of Motion has come up with a package that answers future growth.

"The plan is a two-pronged solution," said Minister of Motion (MiniMo) Eve Even. "First, we're asking the British public to breathe less to conserve resources, then we are going to build a new class of road purely for airliners."

The new roads will be 250yds wide and connect all of the UK's major airports.

Signs of the Times

Road Signs Explained

The Department of Motion is the government agency responsible for Britain's road signs – of which there are tens of thousands – but the whole system has recently had a make-over and now sports new highway signs endorsed by the Ministry of Truth and Other Information, fulfilling its commitments under the Freedom of Information Act to make all signage as explicitly truthful as possible.

Needless to say, this has upset quite a lot of people.

Examples of some of the new signs – and indeed, old signs with new meanings – are reproduced here for your reference.

Explicit direction signage

A12
Lowestoft 15
Shithole 15

WAZOCK SUPERCILIUM

Failed Victorian conurbation with emerging crack problem
(A30)

Twee village where idiotic snobs go to die
A165

Emergency sign

Axis of Evil prohibited (except for goods access)

Signs that are portents of doom

BSE Ahead

Outdated transport infrastructure

Caution: Wrath of God

Red Sea Ahead

Oncoming war stories in centre of road

Copy and paste zone

Beware of tuning forks

Condom caught on fencepost

Freudian symbol: turn on headlights

Signs that you're getting on

Daddy, can I have a bicycle?

Please drive Austin 1300 into lake here

Consult AA road atlas immediately

Road markings

Aircraft lane

Priority lane for parking-based homicide

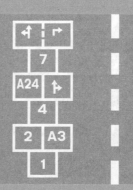

Hopscotch lane

The Train Drain

A Guide to Britain's Railway Infrastructure

1 Ticket Vending Machine Replica of real ticket machine, absolutely correct in every detail, including the fact that it will not dispense tickets. Driven by software that once revolutionized the programming of toasters.

2 Automated Sincere Apology System Computer-generated announcements about how fundamentally shagged the rail system is today. A public-address system is also integrated so that live announcements with unforeseen words and phrases such as "early" or "on schedule" can still be made.

3 Ghost Train Passenger Every railway has a ghost train story, but British ghost train services are often dogged by strikes and the disruption affects passengers caught in the twin limbos of rail travel and expiry. They face a long and fruitless death floating towards any light that takes their fancy. Awayday tickets are not valid on this service.

Way Ou

Architect's Illustration Model As used for original artist's impression of the station, and now retained because he makes everything look fantastically cool. He is 6ft tall, comes condensed for extra effect and is known as Jeff. Budget for Jeff comes from the Black Projects Division of Notwork Rail.

Impenetrable Signalling System An ingenious semaphore-based messaging system principally used to send off-colour jokes and rude observations about Notwork Rail management up and down the country.

The Tracks Due to complex franchising arrangements, the offside rail is owned by a Portsmouth man who bought it at a jumble sale. The nearside rail is owned by RightRail who leased it to LeftRail plc who, in order to promote dynamic, blue-sky environments of risk taking often use it as a stake in back-room poker games at international rail conferences.

UK Rail Information

The UK's fastest train is the "Happy Flier" – a 225 Intercity Express train specially built out of carbon fibre and a titanium-enriched polymer with a super lightweight power engine at each end of a single carriage. However, it achieved a massive speed increase with the addition of two thin red lines painted down the length of the train.

Now, it can reach speeds of up to 208mph, and will actually become airborne from time to time if conditions allow and the buffet does not take on enough pork pies as ballast.

How do I buy a ticket?

You'll be delighted to know that buying a ticket has never been easier: just work out what train you wish to travel on, roll up to the station with 10 minutes to go before it leaves, hand over a large, unmarked briefcase stuffed with notes and you're ready to go. After a brief and frankly unhelpful discussion with a plexiglass shield in a draughty corridor.

What about cheap fares?

Travelling by rail means you can choose from up to 27,000 permutations of tickets, depending on which seats you want and which otherwise harmless weather phenomenon or random route diversion you would like to ruin your journey.

What about advance discounts?

Certain rules apply to advance discount tickets, namely that they are quantum events that cannot be both observed and booked at the same time. They are also subject to the Rail Uncertainty Principle, in which physicists speculate whether or not theoretical trains travelling at the speed of light stretch time behind them in order to offset timetable alterations. Though seemingly academic, this has two important outcomes when calculating Rail Uncertainty for Britain:

- Signalling on the West Coast mainline will have to be significantly upgraded to allow for trains travelling at light speed.

- Trains are strictly theoretical.

> ❝ **Passengers receive regular safety announcements on what different types of scraping noise mean.** ❞

Can I go to sleep?

Yes, of course you can. Sleeping bolt upright in your seat is the efficient way to travel, and ensures that you will arrive wired and antagonistic for your meeting and will therefore get what you want. We pride ourselves on the amount of inefficient bon-homie that can be driven out of even the most bumbling and apologetic executive during one of our rail journeys.

Relax

Settle into short, fruitless snoozes, broken by the insistent sound of tiny cymbals perforating ear drums half a carriage away. Or a chain of jarring, arhythmic beeps from a 1in-wide phone game so apparently immersive that the player has become discon-nected from reality. If all else fails and you really do need to sleep, take a moment to read our soporific, corpo-rate propaganda-zine featuring real stories of railway personnel holding chromium-plated Compliant Employee Awards aloft as if they were the FA Cup. Doze off and be awoken once again by announce-ments about the hopelessly disorganized buffet staff, helpfully amplified via a fuzzbox and delivered through an array of cracked glass speakers.

Rail privatization works

Rail privatization has been so successful in Britain that there are no longer enough rails or modern power units to service the demand.

Shown above is a new rural train service, based on the principle of an engine, powered by a paraffin stove, towing a small number of garden sheds around. Passengers receive regular safety announcements on what different types of scraping noise mean.

Emergency Rail Map

By being British, you explicitly agree to accept a substandard railway system built from a Victorian Meccano set and staffed by people with extraordinary sideburns. Moreover, you are psychologically disposed to levels of blank calm in the face of utter incompetence and ineptitude. Which is where our new Emergency Rail Plan comes in.

During officially designated Rail Emergencies – for instance, a total collapse of the system at the hands of an unexpectedly heavy dew – the agency responsible for failing to run the network – Notwork Rail – has authorized the use of a number of tourist railways, footpaths, pleasure boats, rollercoasters and ley lines to form the Back-Up Railway Network.

In some cases, the use of this network may cause a slight delay, so passengers are recommended to allow an extra six days for their journey and to carry a change of clothing. Also, where a trip includes a section of ley line, customers are reminded to take a Celtic shield, a dead chicken (Kievs not valid for travel) and a Late Perpendicular cathedral with a St. Michael or George dedication. Railcards are not valid unless accompanied with a current Kirlian Photocard with an auspicious aura countersigned by a person of good standing, such as a serving police officer or village shaman.

London Connections

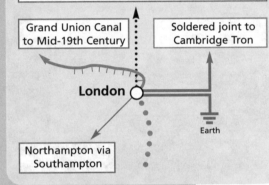

Connecting Rickshaw to Hampstead Garden Village MicroSuburb then onward to back clinic

Grand Union Canal to Mid-19th Century

Soldered joint to Cambridge Tron

London

Earth

Northampton via Southampton

Notes

- ★ Please see blackboard on pier for voyage details.
- C:/> Please check that you are DOS formatted before joining this service.
- Om This service operates along a Geomantic Leyline.
- † Not on Sundays. Ever. Oh, alright then. Maybe.
- ∞ Jenny Agutter Express. Victorianesque bloomers must be displayed on demand.

Quick Tip

For a non-Home Counties version of this leaflet, save time by simply assuming that there are no non-Home Counties versions of this leaflet.

Key to Lines

- ⊙━━ Bluebell Line
- ⊙━━ Nene Valley Steem-ah
- ⊙━━ The Ipswich Train Drain
- ⊙━·━ Symbolic Link
- ⊙···· Public Footpath

- ⊙━━ Trips Around the Lighthouse
- ⊙━━ Anglian Demon Rollercoaster
- ⊙━━ Brighton Tramway
- ⊙ Broadband Matter Transference

Here be dragons

Peterborough · · · · · · · · · · Far Out

Northampton

Cambridge Tron
C:/>

Ipswich Plughole

London

London Parkway

Ferry port link ∞

Om
Southampton

Brighton   Black Rock

✱Needles

✱Portland

Bus Information

Nationalocalbus

Britain's bus network now has the most modern fleet of bus and coaches anywhere in Britain, except in London where they are even newer.

Not everyone at the bus stop is there to admire the vehicles or be aroused by the scintillating gleam of sunlight on the "Please Tender Exact Fare" sign. So here's every citizen's guide to travelling by bus.

How do I catch my bus?

Stand at the bus stop and raise your arm to indicate you would like the bus driver to stop. There is no need to shout "coo-ey"at this stage.

Because buses can travel at up to 14mph, drivers may not always see you in the dizzying blur and you may need to use exotic hand signals to get them to stop. A selection are shown at the top of the facing page.

Always make eye contact with drivers, staring them down to succumb to your overpowering will, while you systematically destroy the covalent bonds between their egos and ids. Please make sure you have the correct change.

Are there any discounts?

Senior Citizens (65+) get a 10% discount when they produce their GreyDay Pass – available to all OAPs who answer questions on Gracie Fields and bring their birth certificate, ration books, biscuit tin and heart-warming tales of being bombed to the adjudicating officer.

Which Ticket?

We offer a full range of tickets to suit almost any purpose.

Return

If you're feeling lucky enough to catch two buses in one day, this may be the ticket for you.

Single

This is for people who have vowed never to return "over my dead body", "until the end of time", or on the same day, whichever is sooner.

A useful ticket for an estranged partner to purchase in a flood of tears as they bitterly choke out the word "single" to a respectfully morose driver.

Please have the exact fare ready or we may not be able to take you to your final destination, further triggering your latent rejection complex and feelings of alienation.

Specialist Gestures
and what they mean

I badly need this bus
Unlikely to work as the driver will regard you as far too needy for bus travel.

I'm making a film
I am only interested in the compositional qualities of the bus. Please pass.

Passenger Power
Unlikely to work unless the destination board reads "Cuba" or "Sheffield".

Thumb
Secret signal enabling free travel on certain buses with rainbows painted on them.

Are there any special seats?

Yes. There are special seats for the old, the infirm and the curmudgeonly. The bus conductor is authorized to beat them with sticks if they attempt to sit anywhere else.

Back seats are reserved for gobby teenagers and the route's Loony-in-Residence.

Before each journey, a secret tombola draw determines where lonely and sexually thwarted passengers who seek furtive skin contact and slight rubbing against other passengers will sit.

More Tickets

Pay As You Go
This ticket enables you to pay for your journey in arrears, with installments becoming due at the end of each fare stage. No messy tickets to handle, no contract, just a minor surgical procedure to install the implant and our Fare Dodger Electrode Harpoon technology and then you are ready to go. After a short convalescence.

You're covered under the Consumer Credit Act 1976 so, if you are not completely satisfied with the quality of your journey, simply return the bus, its driver and passengers to the garage in the same condition in which you received them and owe us nothing.

For Your Assimilation

The use of italic typefaces, slanting logos, the word "express" or service numbers prefixed with an "X" does not necessarily imply increased velocity or the use of futuristic, streamlined bullet-buses.

The representation of a bus or service times in, on, or in close proximity to this leaflet does not necessarily indicate or imply the provision, presence or existential reality of either a bus or a bus service.

Great Britain, Plc

WORK, MONEY AND TAX

CONTENTS

"Wise men make money while fools stick twigs in poo."
Northamptonshire proverb

Introduction

When it comes to financial status and matters of money and wealth, Britons are, by and large, very private people. Indeed, conspicuous display of wealth is as egregious a no-no as the public exhibition of one's genitalia or the freely volunteered confession that you own a Yes album. It just isn't done and, in some cases, may even carry a heavy legal penalty. Britain has many laws surrounding the use of money.

For example, it is illegal to take photographs of money because it is thought to steal the soul of the Queen, which would then lead to the loss of Ravens from the Tower of London and, in turn, the nutritious meals they provide for the so-called Beefeaters. But that is just one of many royal traditions that surround money.

It is often said that Her Majesty does not carry money. It was assumed for many years that, because it included her own likeness, it would have the same effect as giving a dog a handbag mirror and would only lead to confusion. In fact, Her Majesty does carry cash, as well as a special voucher to print more at any high street branch of Prontaprint, just in case.

Royalty aside, it is considered impolite and coarse to enquire of a Briton's financial circumstances, unless you are the chartered accountant

Importance of Money

We all know how important money is to our lives, but how many realize the importance of it to the economy as a whole?

In the last few years, money has become the most significant indicator of all, according to many key economic yardsticks, notably the Chancellor of the Exchequer's Tea Tray of Indicators.

The Tea Tray is Treasury tradition, presented daily to the Chancellor at 3pm along with Navy biscuits and a steaming pot of laudanum tea.

Documents on the tray contain important indices of fiscal fitness like Retail Amazement, Manufacturer Despondency, Business Pessimism About Wholesaler Optimism and the CEO Pissing Forecast. It is on the basis of these documents and the inherent qualities of laudanum and the Admiralty's Bakery, that key economic decisions are made.

Taking pictures of money is illegal in Britain so, instead, we allowed a borderline crack-fiend to play with our Spirograph for an hour, using a number of coloured biros and some fairly suspect Masonic imagery.

Money Alternatives

Some Britons claim that money is purely an arbitrary subjective construct and has no inherent value of its own. So, is this an intelligent deconstruction of fiscal policy? And why not?

Alternative systems exist in outlying hippy communes scattered like pustulent sores across the face of the nation. One such trading system – the world's oldest – is barter.

Barter works on the principle of swapping goods or services, and is the perfect solution for folk musicians and health food shops, which would otherwise have difficulty obtaining real payment for their wares. But, transactions that do not involve eggs, car repair, a short Scottish reel or a pick-up truck full of chicken shit can run into difficulty.

For example, getting your car serviced in the barter system can take a lot of advance planning. It may be months before you track down a mechanic with the kind of serious omelette fetish you need to complete work on your car. And who's to say they won't throw in an unnecessary sword dance to puff up the bill while you're not looking?

of that person, or are commissioning an act of highway robbery when, in either case, it is merely judged as impertinent.

However, you must make an exception if you are required to do so by BBC researchers assembling a feature on the effects of the Budget on a "typical family".

It is a little known fact that BBC researchers are allowed access to all parts of your life in the public interest. But only where that public interest neatly intersects with the BBC's remit to "provide programming of an off-colour, voyeuristic or overtly intrusive nature".

However, the BBC must hold a valid warrant to unpeel your private life, which must then be signed by a senior member of either the High Court or the Dimbleby family.

For the true British gentleman or lady, these are all moot points because the very act of becoming completely British means you aspire to join the aristocracy, and never have to worry about money again.

However, we accept that money – particularly how to acquire it – excites discussion and debate among the populace, and even holds some academic interest for those who have no need of it.

Also, we concede that it can be necessary to top-up inheritances from time to time for certain special purposes, such as the purchase of a folly or the provision of a police bribe to make the sirens stop and the allegations go away. If this applies to you, please turn the page for suggestions on how to make money.

SMUG SUBURBANITES' OUTGOINGS

The Wap family

Yacht wrangling.	**£250,000**
Haircuts.	**£13,000**
Tax them & make them cry.	**85%**

Latest Stuff > **CORRECTION: PM's Jobs Blow, not as stated earlier "Blowj**

Above: The first frame of a BBC *Budgetmania* information panel, seen here as it unpeels the layers of financial privacy from a hapless couple and their soon-to-be taunted children.

Left: How the same graphic appears on Channel 5 or, alternatively, through the bottom of a scratched marmalade jar.

How to Make Money

There are many ways of making money in Britain, but most of them can be grouped into just a few categories

① Employment

The favoured option for most of the workforce, this involves travelling to a building in a town, reading some company memos about productivity or the new pro-active model of customer service paradigm integration, after which personnel are then free to surf the Internet for five hours. All of this is made possible in a furiously competitive world, by the importance of attendance over achievement, in itself a reflection of a classic British attitude. It's not the winning, but the taking part that counts.

④ Public Appointment

Although advertised in Britain's top broadsheet newspapers, the key to winning a public appointment lies in being so close to the centre of power you have no need to read a newspaper at all. You can gauge the relative importance of an official position by the size of its advertisement. For example, a recent vacancy for Chairhuman of the Potato Excellence Council warranted only six lines of copy on the personals page, including the telling phrase "would suit lonely, retired, desperate person with anger or murderous loathing for inferior root vegetables".

➋ Self-employment

This option is typically for people who would like to own some kind of commercial vehicle, such as a small van, and drive it around the ring road while dressed in a boiler suit swearing at cyclists. But it wasn't always like this.

Self-employment of the more glossy kind became very fashionable in Britain in the 1980s at around the same time as the slim-slat Venetian blind. Advertisements of the era featured moodily lit, black-ash offices full of hatchet-faced young professionals in double-breasted suits exchanging conspiratorial glances with one another. The dress code for these meetings always seemed to favour the big suit, New Romantic look, so that everyone resembled a member of Spandau Ballet with a high-yield Personal Equity Plan.

➌ Blue Chip Larceny

The City of London's Square Mile is at the financial heart of Europe and, as such, has always been a vibrant and exciting centre for perpetrating high-value embezzlement.

It offers ample opportunities for the right individual, in a position of trust, to acquire enough money to buy the company they are skillfully siphoning funds away from, and to do it before lunch.

During lunch, expert fiddlers can move entire multinational corporations around the world using a series of holding companies with paper accounts and cardboard CEOs. They often leave a trail of mysteriously abandoned office buildings and burnt-out accountants, which are then hidden in hollow mountains and homes for the fiscally exhausted.

Uncivil Servant

London. Unlimited earnings potential.
Excellent benefits including car, speedboat, microlight, gun.

 ## Are you...

A weak-chinned Oxbridge paedophile with a penchant for mainlining lavatory cleaner and strangling prostitutes?

Hungry for a fast-track career compromising third-world governments and blowing up bridges?

Is your current job holding you back with poor pay and conditions, modest options for growth and not enough access to high explosives?

Do you cherish control of a sophisticated armory of lethal force at the helm of HMFBA – Her Majesty's Fist of Brutal Annihilation?

 ## Do you? Really?

Then you're just who we're looking for. We need a team of outgoing psychopaths who are great at working under extreme pressure. No academic qualifications are necessary, but you need to exhibit enough interpersonal and communication skills to win people's trust shortly before you have them assassinated.

You must also be agile, athletic and fit because at times you will need to run like fuck from the scene of your latest atrocity.

You will work in a chaotic environment, usually of your own making and will meet foreign dignitaries, members of pressure groups and environmental agencies, all of whom you will be required to kill.

Write now

If you've got what it takes – a steely nerve, lots of guts and a slightly dreamy malevolence, we want to hear from you.

Write to us with your CV, or whisper into a nearby table lamp for full details by return of post.

"Your statutory rights are non-effective"
Department of Social Scrutiny
Whitehall • London • SW1

Dealing with Taxes

You have to pay it or the Department of Social Scrutiny will come round to your house with a cricket bat, do you understand? A cricket bat. So what's the friendliest way to proceed?

❶ Find your Tax Office

Your tax affairs are handled by your local tax office, an austere concrete and steel edifice designed by a team of depressed sado-brutalist architects. To discover its exact location, you can either follow pale and harassed-looking office workers in brown polyester suits during the morning rush hour, or use sniffer dogs to track the distinctive aroma of manila envelopes.

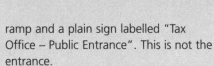

❷ Find the entrance

Government buildings are specially designed to have multiple entrances and exits. This dates back to a cold war policy of modelling official buildings on badger setts, so as to enable the occupants to leave in a timely manner if the building came under threat.

Some of these exits may be located some distance from the main building. A former DHSS office in Beaconsfield featured a tunnel leading to a porcelain door that doubled as a urinal splashback in High Wycombe.

For your purposes, however, you will be more concerned with the doors located on the building. The largest door often has some kind of porch, an access ramp and a plain sign labelled "Tax Office – Public Entrance". This is not the entrance.

This door was used in 1992 for two weeks before a major "Building Realignment Audit", the main recommendation of which was an internal rotation of the building by 27.3°. If you managed to open this door, you would be confronted by a gentleman from High Wycombe relieving himself on your shoes.

3 How to pay

Tax offices are multiple currency agencies. Normally cash is fine, but higher-rate tax payers can also elect to pay with:

- High-value casino chips
- Suitcases of cocaine
- Assassination of troublesome members of Her Majesty's Opposition

4 How we use your data

Your forms lead an interesting life the moment they enter the system. A good example is your P45 – the form you receive after you've pissed your job against a wall. While you worry about your mortgage and the scowling, unsymmetrical faces of staff at the local Jobcentrehassleplus, your P45 begins the kind of exotic journey only pre-packaged Oriental snacks can dream of.

All P45 data is first inputted into an underground computer silo for processing, dispersal and retrieval.

After sorting, the original is sent to Rangoon for I-Ching interpretation by accountants at the As Above, So Below Institute of Tax. After three full moons have elapsed, the original form is burnt in a sealed bell jar and the ashes collected for auditing and mass-spectrometry. The jar is broken against the hull of a ship bearing your tax data, which is then sailed into the Bermuda Triangle.

The last five steps of the process have only ever been attained by computer modelling.

You can find a fuller description of all these processes in the tax office leaflet *"What the Fuck Have You Done With My Tax Records?"*, which is freely available at your local office inside a large, erratically rotating jar of wasps.

5 Now turn the page

APPLICATION FOR MERCY

About your dreary world

PAYE Reference. You can usually find this barcoded on your inner thigh.

1.1

Your nearest Tax Office. This is a tall, grey, windowless building with the aesthetic allure of a box of faeces.

1.2

If you died during the last tax year, tick box 1.3 and seek medical assistance.

1.3 Please ask for the Ouija board version of this form.

About your worst Kafkaesque nightmare

If you answered 1.1–1.3, tick 1.4, ignore 1.5 and estimate the total number of ticks you used on your Tax Return last year. Then add this number to your NI number and write the result in box 1.6 in order to gain access to the Internet component of your Application for Mercy: the Tax Return Text Adventure.

1.4 Tick box 1.4 is withdrawn for existential auditing. For your convenience, the Tax Office have provided a replacement box brought in from a more specialized form.

Anus We hope it does not spoil enjoyment of your regular Tax Return.

1.6

Please log on to www.socialscrutiny.org and shout this number at your screen repeatedly until you are served, and the entire system goes into meltdown.

Typical screen from Tax Return Text Adventure. Your Internet may vary.

```
>>> THERE IS A DOOR MARKED ENTRANCE. N,E,S,W?
>   Push it open
>>> IT WILL NOT PUSH. N,E,S,W?
>   Pull it open.
>>> THERE IS A MAN CALLED TOBY STANDING IN FRONT OF YOU. YOU HEAR A TRICKLING
>>> SOUND N,E,S,W?
>   Give him the form.
>>> UNKNOWN VARIABLE *FORM* TRY *LANTERN*, *SPADE* OR *AMULET OF THOTH*
>>> TOBY IS PISSING ON YOUR SHOES. N,E,S,W?
>   ▓
```

About your uncertain future

■ *Your Worthless Pension*
Tick box 1.7 if you have an annuity or belong to a company pension scheme that has not all been placed on a horse.

7:1

A horse is a large quadruped that is a transient by-product of glue manufacture.

About your pointless drudgery

■ *Your Employer*
An employer is a person you work for in return for luke-warm respect, and a weak promise about your future prospects.

1.∞

Declaration

■ *I declare that*
Although it is my sworn duty as a subject of Her Ladyship The Windsor Queen to defraud the Tax Office, the information I provide on this form is, to the best of my knowledge and belief, a true and accurate account, so help me God. Amen.

1.9

Tick box 1.91 if you are crossing the fingers of your left hand behind your back.

1.91

Tick box 1.9.2 if you intellectually condone decimal non-conformity.

1.9.2

You are going to Hell.

Fill in supplementary pages BEFORE you read this sentence.
Please use blue, black or burnt sienna ink to fill in your Tax Return and not blood, sweat, tears or other symbolic corporeal fluid you may feel is appropriate.

When you have filled in this form, you may tick this box ☐ as a reward. If you tick the box before you have finished all the questions, you may not get any pudding, be sent to your room, or face an Investigations Panel of barking dogs with mechanical claws.

If you have enjoyed this form, please tell us about your friends.

Indolent
Revenue

TRANSITIONAL IRRITATION ALLOWANCE

- This form is used by the Tax Office in order to assess whether or not you should be assessed for eligibility for assessment. This is how we distribute Transitional Irritation. Optionally, this form may also be integrated into a desk-floor interface where there is a proven leg function shortfall caused by, or directly related to, an uneven floor, a leg length mismatch or a non-constructive coincidence of the aforementioned factors.

- If you cannot correct leg function shortfall with this form, please continue on another sheet.

- You may also find the leaflet on Long-Term Personal Irritation Allowances useful. Which, broadly speaking and without constituting a full statement of the law, is why we have not published it.

- /usr/lib/leadpipe/colonelmustard

About your scintillating existence

Your name.
We ask you for your name up to six times on every form in order to unmask instances of poorly planned identity theft.

2.1

Your exact age in seconds
We need this information now in case it later transpires that we needed this information previously.

2.2

Untick box 2.3 if you don't wish to receive special offers from HM Inspector of Taxes or other carefully selected faceless bureaucrats.

2.3 ✔ *This form is property of HM Government and may not be cosmetically sullied.*

Tick box 2.4 if you're happy and you know it and would dearly like to show it.

2.3 *Do not tick if you have already clapped your hands.*

About your happiness

We want you to be pleased with your customer service enquiry. However, if you are not 100% delighted with our service, have frustrated outcome issues, a failure of interpersonal transactional adjustment, or have simply been told to piss off by one of our trained operators, we'd rather not hear about it, thanks. But, we're only human* and will happily provide you with a soundproof cubicle and a loaded shotgun if you feel you need to make a further complaint.

*Does not wholly apply to all staff, to be honest.

About your customer service enquiry

1	2	3
4	5	6
7	8	9

■**Tick 1** to speak to someone from a Department of our choosing.

■**Tick 2** to listen to a 47-second tape loop of bad lounge music.

■**Tick 4** to be connected to a call centre where neon lights flicker at a frequency that enables employee mind control.

■**Tick 3** to have this form posted back to you with a bonus picture question for 5 points.

About your philosophical integrity

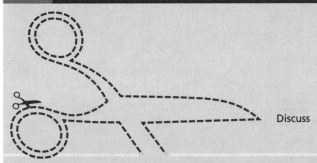

Discuss

Please psychically absorb these paragraphs BEFORE you read them

This form is the property of HM Government and may not be copied, forwarded, stored in a Swedish sideboard or guarded by mechanical dogs without the express written permission of the Secretary of State, the 14th Earl of Bentwaters, his agent, representative or suitable metric alternative, such as an Italian Contessa measuring exactly 1 cubic metre in volume.

The exact specification for Metric Pack Italian Contessas, which was missing from previous versions of this form, was added and then later removed for safety reasons.

The form is now on watermarked bond, with a design depicting the birth of Shakespeare from the mouth of a lion rampant on Boudicca's lap.

The Customer Service Tickpad has been modified and may now be incompatible with your phone. To ensure compliance, buy a compliant phone. Where this is not possible, prise off the zero (0) key from your phone and fill the hole with cement mortar.

*Following this upgrade, you will no longer be able to dial phone numbers with a zero (0) in them, and you may regret reading these paragraphs in a sequential fashion.

Indolent
Revenue

Hooray, you've been fired
Copy for dole-draining scum ★

P45t 1t

For the employer

- *Please fill this form in as you laugh maniacally within earshot of remaining staff furtively cowering in their cubicles.*
- *It will take approximately 0.7 Havana Cigars to complete in full.*
- *You may photocopy and pin this form to a staff noticeboard for the purposes of employee oppression.*

1 Employee ID Chip #
This is often located in a small cavity behind the employee's left ear.

2 Place employee teardrop on treated strip
We need to confirm that your employee interprets your complex use of management euphemisms as dismissal.

3 Bullshit checklist:

Enabling blue-sky platforms for alternative personal growth

Re-focussing Human Resources

Responding to a bijou personnel paradigm

For the employee

1 Reason for your dismissal:

Gross idealism. Tactless flair for your job.

Tested positive for Soul. Too popular and likeable.

Evacuating your colon on your Line Manager's in-tray.

2 Please confirm you have read these clauses in your contract before you rip it up in a final pointless gesture of defiance.

I agree that my pension fund contributions may be temporarily re-allocated to the 4.30 at Haydock Park.

To counter office stationery theft, sniffer dogs sensitive to the aroma of Post-it notes will be deployed at building exits.

In the event of my dismissal, Maoist disavowal and character assassination will form part of the company's grieving process.

★ About this form

Detach this form from your forehead and hand it to your new leader.

You may need this form at an indeterminate time in the middle-future when your tax affairs are investigated by a consortium of spiteful paper-pushing gits in polyester suits and Ford Mondeos.

Please read the notes attached to Part 9 of sub-section B of this and **all other** forms. It will explain what to do next in a patronizing, yet vaguely threatening and authoritarian, manner.

You are not alone.

To the new employer

Hello. My name is

I come from

Please find me a desk and sap my soul for the next ⬜ day/month/year*

For office use only wheeeeeeeeee

114

jobcentrehassleplus

So You've Got Your P45

Hey, chin up. Just because you've lost your job through no fault of your own, there's no need to be all down-hearted or to sink into the hand-to-mouth destitution of cheap groceries and court orders. Not just yet, anyway

It isn't all rejection and despondency, you know, because there's someone who always wants to see you, no matter how much you turn them away or pretend you don't care. That's right, that's us, we're the *Jobcentrehassleplus*.

Jobcentrehassleplus loves you a lot, but knows you're not ready to make a big commitment. We only want to see you once a fortnight – we can do lunch or dinner or, better still, how about a long and demeaning interview?

With *Jobcentrehassleplus* your P45 opens a world of opportunity. Just look at the great services on offer in your nearest branch.

- Each of our centres is equipped with the latest high-tech gear, like paper and biros, and hologrammatic claim forms that enable us to misplace your details in three dimensions at once.

- Every local newspaper in the world with each instance of the word 'job' high-lighted in pink.

- A bank of crashed *Jobsearchmachines* that only show "marketing" jobs in Dorset offering £500,000 p.a. without mentioning it's actually double glazing canvassing, and you will quite rightly go to Hell.

- Staff, now at software version 0.8.3, have had all their bugs – like yawning in the client's face, secretion of mouth corner spittle and tongue-lolling – de-programmed and purged from their operating systems so they can now make up their own rules and misunder-stand regulations for months on end.

British Banking Guide

Currency
The pound rose against the euro, which rose against the dollar, which rose against the yen, which rose against the pound, creating an infinite loop, Escher-style currency illusion.

Shares
Pork Index climbed 15 to Honey Roasted Ham.

Outlook
Sunny spells in West. Turning cold with prolonged outbreaks of monetary breakdown in Far East.

Britain's banks offer a variety of services to their customers, whether they want them or not.

Gone are the days when dreary, wood-panelled High Street branches simply offered safer ways to store money than wrapping it up in greaseproof paper and hiding it in Bakelite wirelesses. All that was swept away in the 1990s, when a new wave of service values and strategic staff lay-offs brought the banks blinking into the dawn of the 21st century.

These days, there are two types of bank accounts. On the one hand, private banks – small, exclusive institutions with the fragrant staff and exotic decor that suit kinky aristocrats, well-heeled metrosexual MPs and other fiscal fetishists. These banks offer a better quality of money with steam-cleaned and sterilized notes and edible, legal-tender chocolate coins freely available in barrels by the door.

The other type are High Street banks, so-called because that is where you'd expect to find their branches. They offer a range of accounts that boil down to two types, business and personal. Levels of service differ widely between the two.

If you are a business customer, your manager will even come to your premises in person to bring you your shrink-wrapped business starter kit. Often tastefully presented in a non-standard, leatherette, 11-hole ring binder, for which you will have to buy a ream of triangular paper and a specialist hole punch, it will open up a world of exotic business stationery you never knew existed.

116

continued on page 120

"freedom"

Jazzbank

a guide for explorers

be free

find freedom

find freedom for your money

A fool and his money are soon parted, runs the old parable. But what about the wise and their money? Can they be parted?

We like to think so. Let's try.

Come to the bank that's tuned into your needs as surely as we're tuned into the one-world zeitgeist of aspirational widescreen zenverts.

Come to us. You'll be impressed by our say-nothing, twisted, 30-second television ad-fables that ooze with vanilla simplicity, as well as displaying the depth of insight and woozy reasoning faculties of a drugged badger.

And all of this with the convenience of a local[1] branch managed by friendly, happy teenagers on work experience.[2]

all free
when you free
all your money

We know how hard it is to keep track of your finances, so we came up with a Business Starter Kit that could be just the thing.

And some burly men to remind you to keep sending us the money.

Your Business Starter Kit includes this attractive 9-hole ring binder, which you can upgrade to 11 holes after approval of your second mortgage and our repossession of your home.

Other pack contents include all sorts of tools to help new businesses: a ninja star remover, a spanner, three starling eggs, a replica Smith and Wesson revolver and a live human hand.[3] The hand is not illustrated, in accordance with section 11 of the Depiction of Quivering Limbs Act, 2004.

Jazzbank Yeah Corporation ("The Bank") licensed to trade on a far-off Indian Ocean island by a military junta, which quietly seized power last Wednesday. Following a fiscal crisis on the island, the interim government liquidated the assets of the bank and changed the official currency to cheese. The value of your investments may go off as well as down. [1] If you happen to live close to Bangalore. [2] Based on survey of surly, pouting adolescents before the merciful disintegration of Westlife. [3] Goods remain the property of The Bank until we have repossessed them. *Designed by Deboit-Donglay-Interbang*

Currency

Sterling rose as the dollar lost at Top Trumps with the euro. Germany turned out to have a higher trade deficit than Ohio, and France trumped DC on cigarette consumption. *See multipurpose fiscalgram below.*

Shares

Shares fell sharply in Baba Pibbly Bluechip after an annual report concluded that they would "not amount to anything if they didn't apply themselves to PE". *See multipurpose fiscalgram above.*

Outlook

Short term – excellent.
Long term – fantastic.
Medium term – very, very bad indeed.
Turn fiscalgram 90° and view via fisheye kaleidoscope.

British Banking Guide (cont.)

Personal customers, too, benefit from the brave new world of British banking.

These days, skilled call-centre staff are ready to talk to you about your finances when you are at your most relaxed, just before your first forkful of dinner. They can also arrange extra services for you, such as the repossession of your home, the removal of doors and the insertion of court orders and bailiffs. Banks can even offer letterbox testing services, supplying a constant stream of cheque-books and leaflets about pet insurance for daily comfort, and reassurance for householders about the mechanical durability and status of their domestic apertures.

Apply for a credit card or get a loan decision within the hour and, while you're waiting, why not talk to them about something else – call-centre staff are trained in conversation, it comes as naturally to them as casual banter about debt consolidation. And all of this with the assured and confident friendliness bestowed upon them by a lilting regional accent and a comprehensive, gruelling 30-minute training video shown during their induction at a roadside motel in Essex.

What modern British banks excel at, however, is their local connections. They can tailor their advice according to where you live. Your bank manager almost certainly lives in this country and knows the unique local conditions that apply throughout Great Britain, Northern Ireland and the overseas dependencies. So, when you phone up your bank, you're straight through to your local branch in Perth, no matter where you live. And one thing you can be sure of with British banks, wherever they may be, they always, always know exactly where you live.

The Author,
Britain: What A State,
The Fountain of Immortality
Londonshire.

NOT A CIRCULAR
YOU ARE FEELING VERY DROWSY

URGENT INFORMATION CONCERNING
YOUR LAST CHANCE TO BE UTTERLY
HOODWINKED IN A NOT ENTIRELY
CONVINCING YET COMPELLING WAY

Holy Shit!

NOW!

YES! YES!! YES!!!*

Dear You,

We have written to you today, in fake biro, because you are one of the 12 million lucky, lucky people our database profiles as fragile enough to sign up for worthless crap just to enter a prize draw that appeals to the self-delusional optimism that's ruined your life so far.

Be the envy of your neighbours when you pull up in your drive in the gold-plated, limited edition, 18-cylinder, 12-speed sports carboat you almost certainly won't win.

What are you waiting for? Isn't the pretend cheque we rigged in the envelope to accidentally show through under your address - the cheque that actually turned out to look more like a food hygiene certificate - good enough for you?

Affix the YES!!! sticker to the back of the YES!!!! envelope and fill in the reply-paid Sworn Affidavit enclosing some skin for DNA matching and some product or other will be yours to keep, no matter how many times you try to send it back.

Examine this majestic thing in your home for ten days. Admire its packaging, and the mindless dedication of its creators. If you don't agree that it is a handsome addition to your life, simply return it to a PO Box in Swindon where your lack of commitment and angry correspondence will be charitably ignored for as long as it takes to send you more thingamajigs that reinforce the futility of your thwarted materialism.

Act now: we know where you live.

* No

My most honoured friend,
My late husband was Mr Tomias
Champagne, Head of International
Finance in the Nigerian Worthless
Crap Bank in Lagos. He was roofless-
ly assassissassinated by paramili-
tary factions of the CBM — the well-
known Societé Contré Bibliotheque
Merde. I am his destitute widow,
under house arreste and facing a
life without glossy books to lay on
my occasional furniture.

I have discovered recently that he
left $25 millione in prize draw
funds in my name and I contact you
now to ask for kindness in helping
me recover the seven (7) numbers I
need to open safety depositing box.

Here are the three numbers I have:

RIP-53NDM3M0N3Y
OFF-L0750FM0N3Y
CON-8UYM34H0U53

I now need the last four which, as
luck would have it are hidden in
your bank account number, sort code,
fax number and best chequebook sig-
nature. Please forward to this poor
old widow in the special pre-paid
envelope provided and you can be
sure to get considerable just
desserts from helping me with this
deal.

Your very honourable friend,
Mrs Champagne

Previous prizewinners

MQ Bicester
I never win any-
thing, not since I
accidentally
superglued my
hand to this
cake. I was about to saw
my hand off at the wrist with
this breadknife when you rang
to tell me I had won a Reverse
Bakery Operation.

DFS Toss
When I won your
Prize Draw, I
escaped from the
drab world of
business clip-
photo modelling and
was able to pursue a career as a
close-up porn double. Not at all
bad for a guy who left school
with only a Grade 2 CSE in
Holding a Telephone.

AWOL Swindon
I must admit, when
I first heard about
this prize draw, I
was sceptical.
Then I realized
that I was the one organ-
izing it, so I cashed all the
cheques and ran away with the
money. Thank you all so much
for your funny letters and
phone calls. Bye for now.

SOCIAL
SCRUTINY

Coming of Age
THE MATURE BRITISH DEMOCRACY

CONTENTS

"I put it to you that I put it to you and will continue to put it to you."
The Bad Barristers of Hampshire Society motto

A Quick Constitutional

We're well aware that arguments on the subject of the British constitution can be as shrill and tiresome as a man from Birmingham criticising different grades of hardboard, so we promise that we won't go all heavy on you. And we won't start talking about your constitutional rights either, and would urge everyone else to keep their mouths shut as well.

It is widely – and erroneously – reported that Britain does not have a constitution, but this is both erroneous and wrong because, as the cradle of democracy itself, Britain has the constitution of a slightly elderly man. Great things are certainly in our past, but perhaps we should have written some of them down and shouldn't go banging on about them so often.

As it is, the bits that were written down – the Magna Carta and the writs of habeas corpus, for instance – were done an awfully long time ago. And, like the cloudy and slightly hallucinatory memories of the piss-stained old man that is the United Kingdom, nobody wants to hear about these ancient, handwritten texts any more. A brief description of their indispensibility, along with the government's plans to introduce modern versions that will be clearly typed in Helvetica, follows over the page. We can assure anyone who holds a copy of these documents that they can *now* be safely thrown away. They won't be needed again.

Voting Irregularities

Most people over 18 in Britain are eligible to vote except peers of the realm, prisoners, members of the Royal Family and certified lunatics. The department also proposes that the vote be withdrawn from the following, based on their contribution to society.

- **Devoted fans of the rock group Marillion**
  For reasons of style.

- **Dinner party socialists**
  Purely to oppress them.

- **The cast of the dreary BBC soap opera *EastEnders***
  For bumming-out Christmas with their tragic storylines year after fucking year.

- **Everyone involved in the production or commission of mid-morning television programming**
  The manufacture of expanded polystyrene for the brain should not go unpunished.

 The next BBC *Election Night* designs will feature the paranoianometer – a graphical representation of how much the new government is out to persecute you, the man or woman in the street.

Your responsibilities

This is a legal document. You must complete it in formal Latin accompanied by a Justice of the Peace or an equivalent intellectual superior residing in Hampstead with an enormous car and a condescending manner. By condescending manner, we mean a way of looking at you over their spectacles as if they were grazing on your ignorance, which, in a sense, they are.
Pluribum et nominus cafe latte del monte.

Hold the King James Bible with your left hand, stand on one leg and repeat the following phrase.
Sub judice ab incunabilis magna parmigiano.

This document is your solemn oath to be oppressed, please do not scratch your arse.
Deus fax machina fiat cinquecento hallelujah gloria estefan.

Please fill in your unique base 64 identifier in the spaces below

Letter	Number	Number	Symbolic cypher	PGP Key checksum	Vowel	Consonant	Hieroglyph

Please enter guilty plea in the checkbox provided
You have a right to remain compliant.

Do you wish to hear about additional rights available for purchase?

☐ Yes! Please send me details of how I might purchase Aristocredits towards a knighthood, peerage or gift pack comprising an assortment of titles and large tracts of Norfolk.

☐ Yes! Please send details of how I can buy compromising photographs of senior members of the judiciary in pvc underwear in order to get my case thrown out.

☐ Yes! I would like to mount a legal challenge to my impending incarceration. Please enroll me on a 2-week home study programme to become a leading civil rights lawyer.

Your Rights – UK Guarantee

If you are not utterly delighted with your Britishness, we want to know right away. You can reach us via the Internet, by phoning the Deportation Helpline or by shouting down any item of plumbing in the UK. Your cries for mercy may be recorded for staff training purposes. Your statutory rights remain non-effective.

Habeas Corpus 2006

In line with its remit to streamline the processes of law and order, the Department of Social Scrutiny has signed off a number of improvements to the rights and responsibilities of living in Britain.

One such over-complex principle is that of habeas corpus, which, in layperson's terms, simply means "having a body" – specifically, the police or other agent of retribution bringing your body before a court so you can be punished for wickedness or unpleasant behaviour. Behaviour you are almost certainly responsible for, given that you are appearing in a court of law.

The department felt that this represented an unnecessary duplication of effort and has concluded it is merely necessary for you to "have a body" in order to have the full and withering bifocal glance of justice imposed upon it from afar.

To these ends, the department has produced Habeas Corpus 2006, which crucially updates the age-old presumption of innocence into something more fitting in the Eternal Moment of Danger we find ourselves in. Habeas Corpus 2006 has been enshrined in a new document – one for every UK citizen – which outlines the responsibilities of occupying a British body.

The tear-out document (*left*) takes the form of a customer guarantee for consumers of the United Kingdom – a non-transferable End-User License Agreement outlining what purposes your Britishness may be used for, what to do if you find your nationality is malfunctioning and how you can purchase additional rights from us.

Magna Carta 2006

The Department of Social Scrutiny is to issue consultation documents on a new iteration of the Magna Carta, one rewritten according to current best practise guidelines as posited in the Bletchley Report on Specialist Lingual Interface Methodology.

This modal reiteration of the document presents a unique facilitation juncture to assess the linguistic possibilities of anglophonic text modes in relation to the original Magna Carta.

Copies of this statement are also available in Welsh and in English.

The new document is to be prepared at departmental offices in West Sussex and, in keeping with nomenclature guidelines, will be known by the new name of the Bognor Carta.

LOCAL PARTISAN NEWS

Load of old wank ➤

Voters ready to "deal with" witches p4

OUR WONK CAN WIN

THIS WAS THE MOMENT THAT Barbara Wonk's hard work to save St. Apathia's Road Post Office finally paid off. Only minutes after the bulldozers left, the council agreed to preserve the vital community resource for all time.

Jubilant campaigners (left) jubilated. "The people have spoken," said Barbara, "and I have an assurance that the Post Office will stay exactly as it is for at least the next week, or until a skip becomes available to move the rubble, whichever is the sooner. I think we can safely say that this vital amenity is now beyond threat."

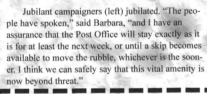

Are you a local busybody coordinating curtain twitching for the neighbourhood from your vantage point at an entrance to a suburban cul-de-sac? Would you like to help the New Libservatives? for a few hours a week to promote someone else's unctious perspective for a change?

Write to Barbara Wonk c/o The Demolished Post Office, FREEPOST, St. Apathia, enclosing a lock of your hair and an item of sentimental value.

Name...

Address ....

Approximate Denier Value of Net Curtain ....

Youth Guide to Voting

ELECTIONS ARE GROOVY!!!

Every five years (four years, if sooner) Britons vote for a candidate to represent them as a Member of Parliament in a General Election.

The largest party forms a government, while the runners-up declare that it's not the winning that's important, but the taking part and, as a direct consequence, fire their leader for taking part. It's just like the hit parade.

With this in mind, it's important that everybody votes, so we have compiled this handy guide for the first-time voter. So, put down your pop discs and *Melody Maker* and let's go.

First, you must find your **Polling Station** (in Scotland it is called a **Polling Place** in order to be pointlessly distinctive) to vote. Unless you live in one of the more advanced constituencies, there is not usually a bar provided.

Once you are inside, and have shown your poll card or given your name to an official – identifiable by the aura of a person who hangs around magistrates courts as a hobby – you will be given a ballot paper and may vote in one of the cubicles provided. Selection of a cubicle follows the same etiquette as the gentleman's urinal code, and you should always vote in a booth not adjacent to one already in use. Similarly, it is not always necessary to wash your hands unless your aim is poor or you make a mark down the side.

You must make a cross composed of two strokes against the candidate you wish to vote for. Do not tick, draw a smiley face, spray your tag or staple your latest flier to the ballot. You really don't want any of the parties at your party. See panel to the right to help you identify where to post your vote. You do not need a stamp.

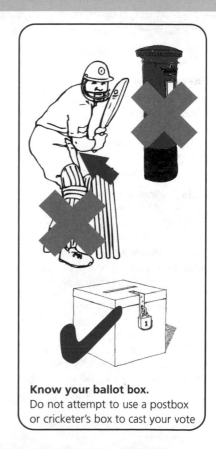

Know your ballot box.
Do not attempt to use a postbox or cricketer's box to cast your vote

 A typical election leaflet from the New Libservatives. Under UK election law, the Royal Mail is not only obliged to distribute leaflets but also to deliver warm dog turds and next door's post to your hallway floor.

Power From the People

Democracy is often personified as a somewhat retarded old gentleman neglected by his busy, monomaniacal children and left to rot under a canal bridge drinking turps and shouting "I used to be important you know, I used to be somebody", but that's not the whole story – and any resemblance to the circumstances of Harry Bladder, father of the Minister of Truth and Other Information, Alan Bladder, MP, is purely circumstantial.

These days, democracy is a much more dynamic process, and the way that process functions is a very long way indeed from that stupid old man.

0915 Focus group
All new policies are discussed by a focus group of senior directors of multinationals – also known as the Cabinet. This session of informal bribery is followed by an adjournment in the Government Liquor Cupboard.

0925 Cabinet meeting
Results from the focus group are reviewed. Members of the Cabinet who expressed weakness or reservations are prevented from returning from the Liquor Cupboard. The policy is passed. Everything else is pissed.

1000 Transparency review
The decision is passed to the Cabinet's Transparency Review Section, which meets in a locked basement reached through a doorway leading from a secret platform in an abandoned Tube station 300ft below an MOD base on a super-node of a secret Wiltshire ley line. Its purpose is to subject the policy to transparency tests. A version of the policy is printed on cling film in order to detect any opaqueness. A successful test of transparency is, therefore, one where nothing is seen.

1100 Tendering process
Once the decision has been determined by the Senior Determinator, a rigorous tendering process begins, integrating the various criteria of value-for-money, standards conformity, best practise guidelines, legal safeguards, cost-benefit analysis and the colour of the regulator's logo.

1110 Tender awarded
In a dark corner of a major London railway terminus.

1120 Payment of contractor
Civil servants are dispatched with holdalls full of cash, using directions written on edible rice paper to the location of a dead letterbox agreed with the contractor in advance.

1135 Contractor goes bankrupt
A carefully researched corner of the Insolvency Act not only allows directors to start another business within 15 minutes, but also to receive OBEs for services to British embezzlement.

1210 Cloning of civil servants
The new policy generates a huge work load. Civil servants become unable to keep up with the demands of office life, which are, broadly speaking, Internet surfing and distributing jokes by email that meekly reinforce sexual stereotyping in a non-confrontational manner. To keep up with their sacrosanct duties, the extension of sheep-cloning experiments to bureaucrats is authorized by government. A breakthrough is announced at 1217.

Behind the Scenes

The decision-making process is a highly complex one, and couldn't be achieved without the mind-less dedication of the following unsung heroes.

Name: **Carmen Spann-King**
Position: *Under Secretary of State*

Duties: Submits to dominant parliamentary committees on constitutional affairs, but is most frequently tied up in controversial briefs on strict regulatory frameworks.

Name: **Sir Iain McGolly-Gosh**
Position: *Vice-assistant to the Deputy Permanent Private Under-Secretary.*

Duties: Adjusting tie, agreeing with absolutely everything so nobody will catch on that he delegates the very few duties he has to the Cabinet toilet cleaner, the Deputy Assistant Vice-secretary of State for Porcelain Management.

Name: **Lord Aubrey Bombed**
Position: *Parliamentary Party Head*

Duties: Deals with procurement of supplies for party functions.
Caveat: This man is not actually a member of the Cabinet Office, but is great fun to be around, whoever he is.

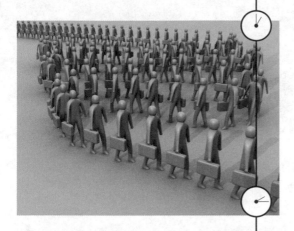

1300 Consultants arrive

The government brings in consultants to manage the process of bureaucrat cloning that will enable the policy to be implemented. A new IT system experiences "teething troubles" when it creates a race of super powerful mail-room androids that take a hard-line policy enforcement initiative, and start to "delete" people instead of posting them consultation documents.

1415 Injunction

Relatives of the deleted obtain a High Court injunction ordering the consultation process to be stopped.

1430 Court challenge

The policy is challenged in court by a consortium of Bolshevics who claim that the government is out of touch with ordinary people. Compelling evidence is offered – of the Prime Minister wearing slacks in a discotheque – the judge rules against it.

1540 Listening

The government listens and the policy is saved by a procedural branding arrangement. It is called something else. The families of the deleted demand a public enquiry.

1600 Government enquiry

A powerful government enquiry is launched by the government into the workings of the Cabinet. The Cabinet is hauled before the enquiry team, made up of the directors of multinationals that sit on the Focus Group that, in turn, make up the entire Cabinet.

1630 Conclusion

A number of officials are reprimanded, presentation issues are discussed and the electorate is found wanting.

Can You be Bothered?

We ask you a few seemingly unrelated, subtle psychometric questions on apathy, anarchy and politics. You answer them and add up your score for the result. Simple.

Points to remember

- Either George Orwell or Winston Churchill probably said something really important and possibly witty about apathy, but we really can't be bothered to look it up right now.

- Anarchy literally means *spider without legs*.
- Apathy is now available as a degree-level course. To apply, simply pick up the phone and sigh to an operator.

1. When politicians come to canvas for your vote, do you?

a Get your mates to hold the crypto-fascists down as you superglue "Enemy of Planet Earth" rosettes to their foreheads? **5**

b Invite them in, give them a cup of tea and talk to them at length about local issues like the dog-turd situation and the closure of St. Crispin's Centre for the Voluntarily Wasted? **2**

c Nod politely as you work out a way of asking them if they can pop down the shop to buy you some chocolate and Rizlas? **0**

2. Plans are published to build a toxic waste dump in what is currently your kitchen. Do you?

a Compliantly move into the lounge on the condition that the contractors make your dinner? **2**

b Start a pressure group to resite the facility in the kitchen of a poorer family who will be grateful for the jobs, and the wider economic benefits brought by the toxic waste industry? **4**

c Make a protest camp with aerial walkways joining the cooker hob with the top of the kitchen cabinets, while teams of expert tunnellers barricade themselves into the oven and washing machine? **6**

3. An abattoir for a major supermarket ritually humiliates turkeys for fun before they are killed for Christmas. Do you?

a Cook the meat a little longer to remove the bitterness? **0**

b Break into the supermarket one night to liberate the frozen turkeys. **4**

c Have a word with the contractors operating the toxic waste dump in your kitchen and mention you "feel like chicken tonight". **1**

How did you score?

11-15 Anarchist

It's obvious that you are a shifty and deceitful, tree-hugging trouble maker with clear issues of personal hygiene to work through, a look-at-me hairstyle that marks you out as a clown, and a gittish knack of over-gesturing with your hands in an effort to look reasonable when you are forced to explain yourself to the authorities.

Confused by a combination of recreational fungi abuse and bewilderingly sub-sonic bass loops, your beliefs that Terence McKenna was an alien, or that the world can be saved through the medium of dance music, are sadly too simplistic and incredible for even George W. Bush to believe.

If you devoted less time to dancing like a helicopter, had a good shave and spent your trust fund more wisely on better drugs, you would quickly turn into the hedonistic scum you so despise.

6-10 Partly Political

Your endearing, misguided belief in democracy is touching but flawed. On the one hand, you are a committed local campaigner, tirelessly fighting to save services available within 100m of your lounge. On the other hand, you are a selfish twit tirelessly fighting to close all the other facilities to keep your taxes low, or to enable your property to rise in value by £1000 before lunch is served.

Your children are important to you, which is why you drive them the 67yds from your home to their classroom in a bullet-proof, half-track Mercedes Benz Humvee, slowing down only to drive over the still-twitching carcase of that "busy-body lollipop bureaucrat".

You flicker between states of apathy and anarchy on a daily basis, but your pattern of thought is dictated by one factor: Is it in my backyard?

0-5 Apathetic

Congratulations on being politically interested enough to accommodate four mouse-clicks into your busy, believe-nothing lifestyle. You must be feeling very proud of yourself.

However, you are still a lazy, mindless, facile blob of animal mash who subsists on a spoon-fed diet of tabloid opinions and daytime soap opera. As an evolutionary measure, your tepid consciousness, unable to maintain political thought, assumes a holding pattern based on the opinions of the last sexually attractive person who wasn't physically ill in your presence.

As a consequence, any convictions that make it to the cerebral cortex of your brain can be easily swamped by the dizzying cocktail of glandular secretions triggered by something as low-level, and apparently pointless, as a cheese and pickle sandwich.

Well done: it's people like you who make this country what it is.

Stop Press... Stop Press

We interrupt your perusal of this tome, to bring you an urgent security alert.

Code Red Ocelot Alert

Introduction
by Sir Edward Bicycle, MP, QC, KFC, DFS

The government's robust attitude to the Combined Forces of Evil hasn't all been a bed of roses, you know.

In our war against these forces, we have inevitably upset some people along the way and now they would like to kill you in ways too painful to explain at length in this short pamphlet.

This may seem unreasonable at first, but you will soon get used to it and quickly realise that there's simply no point in whining about it any more.

So, I urge everyone to control their hysteria, go quietly into their homes and follow the very worthwhile advice in this leaflet.

From this point on, I will be in my bunker, so, cheerio for now!

Sir Edward
xx

Ed (Sir)

Do Nots & Don'ts

- Always obey the instructions of police officers, even if they appear far younger or less intelligent than you.

- Before you hide under a table to protect yourself from a blast wave, check the table conforms to British Standards N-uc134r for use as a temporary shelter.

- Fasten all doors and windows to ensure that your neighbours can not hear you screaming, "We're all going to die."

Now look over there ⟶

Stop Press... Stop Press...

Emergency Numbers

Make a note here of any emergency numbers you may need during the emergency, in the event of another emergency.

The Lead-Shielded Pizza Delivery Co. Ltd
. . . .
NHS Direct 24-Hour ringing tone
. . . .
International Rescue – Thunderbird 2
. . . .
Nostradamus Forecasting, plc
. . . .
Others
. . . .

. . . .

Stay tuned to the electric wireless for emergency government programming during the current state of emergency.

Radio GB 1984 kHz 999 m

9.30 AM The Archers

Eddie brings home a vial of Anthrax he bought from Baggy, but Clarrie isn't best pleased.

12.00
How Clean is Your Bomb?

Channel 4's Kim and Aggie get their feather dusters out on yet another dirty bomb contamination zone.

12.30 PM Foes

The One Where They Board All the Windows Up and Hide Under the Stairs.

Reception notes

Radio GB is available only on long wave and in glorious Britannic stereo on VHF/FM. We recommend listeners arrange for the installation of a roof aerial to enjoy our full programme of martial music and worrying news. The all-clear will be broadcast in surround sound, followed by a play about Northern Ireland to let you know everything is back to normal.

Now finish reading •

SOCIAL
SCRUTINY

Dunmoanin'
THE BRITISH RETIREMENT EXPERIENCE

CONTENTS

Congratulations on your retirement.
Pension? What pension?

"A long walk off a short pier" (1986)
Peter Wenk, DoSS Artist in Residence

Introduction

Britain, in common with the rest of Western civilization, has what is known as an aging population. This means that not only are all of us getting older, but also that none of us are getting any younger.

The knock-on effect of the tendency of all of us to carry on living is that we have more time at the end of our lives for pottering.

Pottering is universal. It ranges from a little gentle gardening or light domestic maintenance to full-blown monomaniacal interests and hobbies, like amassing an enormous collection of ⅜in Whitworth-thread screws and then organizing them according to their importance and function. It includes looking at road atlases, but never going anywhere. There are various fascinations with the food-storage possibilities of advanced tupperware and, most alarming of all, an interest in collecting ceramic figurines of the kind lavishly advertized on the back covers of the Sunday supplements.

The pottering stems from suddenly being let loose with your time, and filling your days accordingly with a set of pointless yet self-contained, satisfying tasks. The long-term aim is to collect enough objects to necessitate the purchase of a card index or, for the more technically minded, a database program.

When Can You Retire?

This is something of a grey area, appropriately enough. As the population ages and there is less "fresh meat" available, pensioners will be increasingly co-opted from pharmacies, where they currently hang around all day talking about their piles, into productive work. So long as it doesn't involve long hours of sitting down or leaning on hot radiators.

The official retirement age is 62½, that being the average of 60 and 65 for women and men respectively before it was challenged in some meddling European court as being unequal. That single judgement could be the reason why men approaching retirement – and now facing 30 months extra of brain-buggering retirement drudgery and lawn-mowing duties – are so Europhobic.

 Before becoming Artist in Residence at DoSS, Peter Wenk was an art critic, but was struck by lightning while maligning Glyndebourne for the *Daily Telegraph*. He now cannot stop reviewing the world around him.

With all that time on their hands, the retired also have a tendency to gather, in the way that pied wagtails do, in sunny spots with puddles. The lure of the failed seaside resort is overwhelming.

Large flocks of feral senior citizens can be seen anywhere with a pier or promenade and many resorts specifically cater for the aged, laying on extra public conveniences, rum-tiddly-tum music and a brand of showbusiness that's frankly best avoided.

For those pensioners who do not actually live at the seaside, the lure is still inescapable. Mr and Mrs Lovely have their priorities for a day's sightseeing. Mrs Lovely is drawn by the promise of a draughty stroll down a godforsaken promenade, while Mr Lovely simply wants to discover the source of the A12, as looked up in his road atlas the night before.

Apparently, there is an original 1950s signpost at the spot, and he wants to take a photo of it to put on his website dedicated to the Primary Route Network. Such is the whirlpool of fun presented by the seaside, from which there is no escape. It will suck each and everyone of us in one day.

Once Mr and Mrs Lovely are home, it's back to gardening and cataloguing the Whitworth-threaded screws again, accompanied by an overarching sense of resigned bitterness against the modern world.

Beside the Seaside

Long past the best years, grey and slightly damp? A façade of faded glory still echoing with the laughter of long-gone happy days?
Then you'll feel right at home at the British seaside.

Are You Alright, Dear?

The DoSS guide for the temporally challenged

The first place to turn if you're worried about money, home security or removing stains from your pelmets and antimacassars*

* Will require additional leaflet

Home Security

As *Crimewatch*'s Nick Ross will almost certainly tell you, a lot of people make a lot of money out of scaring old people, so don't fall into the trap. Secure your home against midnight stranglers, prowling wolves and organ-transplant thieves and, please, don't have nightmares.

Cut down on heating bills
And improve security by not removing the front wall of your home.

Do not let strangers in
It's no coincidence that *stranger* and *strangler* are almost spelled the same way.

Cooking smells
Most burglars are familiar with the technique of using timers to turn lights on and off. By using the oven timer to bake cakes through the night and playing a never-ending tape loop of *The Archers* theme tune, you can disorientate and deter burglars by making them believe it is actually the middle of the day.

Improve your dog
Increase its apparent fierceness by dressing it in a slashed-up tartan dog blanket, and lower the frequency of its adenoidal yap by fitting a baritone bark enhancer or sub-woofer.

The Chimney
Chimneys are now a favoured route into a home. Keep a fire lit at all times, and do not leave mince pies and sherry on the mantlepiece.

The Shed
If you need to summon help in the event of a burglary, you can usually find the gentleman of the house in here, fiddling with a broken toaster.

The Lawn
Fill lawn sprinklers with undiluted hydrochloric acid, and wire up to a motion detector to instantly dissolve burglars, next door's cat and any tree branches that haplessly stray over the boundary.

The Garage
Secure your garage by filling it to the top with soil.

Be alarmed
Burglars are alarmed by burglar alarms, but many have learnt how to disconnect them so, if you have one fitted, make sure you secure it by fitting a further burglar alarm to its cover, securing the additonal alarm by wiring it to the first.

Help with Your Twilight Years

The Department of Social Scrutiny is committed to making you feel safe and cared for in the all-too-short years before your eventual death. To that end, we are proud to offer you the chance of registering with our free Pensioner Appraisal Programme, which gives you, the senior citizen, the chance to give us the benefit of your opinions on public services, as well as how things don't taste like they once did and why the war was so much fun. Just fill out the form on the right and send it back to us, enclosing some boiled sweets and your current pension book.

Don't worry, we'll send your pension book straight back to you, after we have verified your age and played a few sessions of Unreal Tournament Death Squad on the office network.

Each and every registered pensioner gets a free packet of damp petticoat tail shortbread to threaten their grandchildren with, an upgraded funeral plan and enough Winter Fuel Bonus to warm their home to 140° Fahrenheit. You might think that that's a bit parky, but at least it's warm enough for you to take off the immersion heater jacket you put on by mistake when you went to the wrong cupboard last April.

These days, pensioners are making the most of their years left, so let us help you help us wring the last ounce out of yours – join up now to be appraised.

Pensioner Survey

- This form is intended to field your views on issues affecting you, the wise old owl, as well as senior citizens in general. Please find a wing-backed, badly faked Queen Anne electric ejection armchair to complete this form in, and don't forget you've left the oven on.

- Please complete this form in the same haphazard inky scrawl you use for your 28-year-old grandson's birthday card with a picture of a fucking yacht on it. If we cannot read it, we will come round to your house, talk very loudly and accidentally sit on your dachshund.

Your Name
You can find your name printed on the front of your pension book or threatening letters sent to your home by an unjustly militant utilities company.

What is the most exciting thing about being a pensioner?

☐ New plans to link my stairlift into the national rail network.

☐ Telling strangers about my haemorrhoids.

What is your opinion of the NHS?

☐ It's marvellous, I always look forward to being unwell and meeting new people.

☐ They're not doing anything about my legs. Did I mention my haemorrhoids?

For the purposes of identification, please provide a print of your dentures
Do not bite the book directly.

Remove teeth. Remove any traces of ham sandwich on dentures. Press into supplied ink pad and stamp impression in box.

Replace dentures. You may notice a faint black arc around your next sandwich.

Please sign the declaration
I am just a poor, lonely old pensioner a little out of step with contemporary society with an unreasonable love for small, pointless items of pottery and ghastly ceramic figurines for the mantelpiece, as well as coach tours of diseased seaside towns. Please don't take my pension away.

Sign

Date
Hint: it is no longer 1947.

Your Bill

BEHEMOTH UTILITIES PLC

We never, ever forget

MR & MRS LOVELY
DUNROAMIN
FORTFOR
YEW
IN WW2

Fucking pay up now

Utility Used	**£547.00**
Standing charge	**£40.00**
VAT £547.00 @ 5% rounded to next fiver	**£30.00**
Total due	**£687.00**

A discretionary tip has been discreetly applied

Please do not fold this counterfoil. The barcode will charge you double.

HOW WE WORKED OUT YOUR UTILITIES BILL

Your Meter Readings
Your meter was last read by us on the 16 December 1964. You just can't get the staff.
The meter reading was   1457 $^3/_{16}$ Cubic Furlongs of utility.

Customer supplied reading
12 March 2005   1459 $^3/_{12}$ Cubic Furlongs of utility.
15 June 2005   1549 $^7/_{19}$ Cubic Furlongs of utility.

Converted to MetaAngstroms (MA)
Utility Used   12,034.88930153 MA

Adjustment for Julian Calendar and cable erosion
Converted to Gigis (G)
Utility Used   10 G @ £50.00 ea = 750 Euro

Converted to UK pounds   £547.00 + VAT + Tip.

PAYING YOUR UTILITIES BILL

At any bank: Except yours, of course.
At a Post Office: With all the warmth and human generosity you can muster in the face of staff specially picked for their outright hostility and overt sighing.
Home Banking: After you have mastered six combinations of pass phrases, PIN, customer numbers, password hints, birthplace, your dog's inside leg measurement and your father's maiden name.

PROBLEMS PAYING?

If you find payment difficult, it could be that you are just not concentrating hard enough, or you may have payment difficulties which will affect the whole tone of our relationship with you. Please tell us. We can arrange to fit slower utility taps to minimize your use. Or you could try Pay-As-You-Go-Along, where we bring around a jar of gas, some water, some stored electricity and a telephone conversation every day. Cash on delivery.

Further Information

This leaflet is also available in a version featuring extra large print, as well as a CAPITAL LETTER SHOUTING VERSION.

If you would like a copy of either of these leaflets, please write to us at the address below. You should be aware, however, that each of these leaflets is just over 2m in height and printed on much thicker paper to carry the extra weight of the letters. This may have an adverse impact on pensioners with reduced upper arm strength.

Issuing office/authorized dealer

Whitehall • London • SW1

We are currently working on a solution to this dilemma, which will involve a visit to your home by an interactive theatre company, which will initiate an oral discourse and collect answers to the questions. Before applying for a visit, please make sure that your ceiling joists are suitable for anchoring a trapeze mechanism, and be ready to give them a fantastic round of applause.

The Department of Social Scrutiny

Dear Sir/Madam
We write to inform you of your official pension forecast.

As a British pensioner, you know the value of evenly dividing cake to ensure that everyone gets a slice. Well, in a similar way, your pension is part of the government's Victoria Sponge of Expenditure. In short, there is only enough cake to go around.

Fortunately, as a British Pensioner, you also know all about moaning and this is one instance where you will be able to use your whole OAP skillset to great effect.

To go back to our teatime analogy, if you give one person too much cake there will only be a few crumbs left for everybody else, and this is what has happened to your pension. The cake stand is empty and your self-flagellating moaning acceptance of this fact is one of the things that makes Britain Great.

YOUR PENSION

£0 per week.

As you know, the government has overhauled the pensions system in order to allow more flexibility in the provision of pensions and the distribution, as it were, of the cake. Having now divided up the sponge, it has been decided that you cannot have any cake because you and many of your kind are simply not photogenic enough to be linked in any way to a government policy.

I have, or rather, a huge mainframe computer has, enclosed a leaflet with helpful advice to pensioners. The computer trusts it will be of use.

Yours faithfully,
The computer.

The Perfect Lounge

1 **Net curtains** A two-way interrogation device to the outside world. Observe the comings and goings unseen from behind the secret veil. Before infra-red scopes were invented, British police fitted net curtains to their car windscreens during surveillance missions.

2 **Pocket-sized hound** A non-challenging micro-dog should be at the centre of every pensioner's life. Of above normal intelligence, which, as any dog-owner will tell you, means that it is practically capable of learning the Cyrillic alphabet, the hound is smart enough to use its owner's love as a bargaining chip to obtain more gourmet dog food.

3 **Family photographs** Pictures of nearest and dearest in a prominent place to show off to visitors, as well as a visual clue to who's getting the lion's share of the will. An over-abundance of cat pictures means that you are not getting a penny.

4 **Antimacassars** You have to have a good reason to add an extra level of complication to the idea of a chair, but antimacassars are useful when you wish to prevent the unfortunately necessary tide of slovenly tradesmen from relaxing too much in your home, stating, as they do, that you value the furniture more than their company. If you are boiling yours in the wash, simply declare "my, you have filthy hair", and remove all cushions to ensure they remain stiffly perched on the seat edge.

5 **Ornamental knick-knacks** The consciously cluttered look reflects a lifetime of collecting things for every pensioner's dream home, one that is hollowed out of an enormous block of mahogany and containing more gold than Fort Knox.

6 **Mantelpiece** You can reveal a lot about your subconscious mind with the contents of your mantelpiece, so much so that some people pronounce it "mental piece".

Your Guide to the National Health Service

Health Worry Direct

Felt a strange buzzing sensation in your throat and decided you must have St Vitus Tonsillitis? Or maybe your feet smelled funny, and you didn't get around to washing them before you jumped to the conclusion that they must be "rotting from the inside out" because you have contracted a rare foot-based form of the Ebola virus called Pedalo?

If you're the kind of hypochondriac that researches your next disease on the Internet and then bungs up your doctor's waiting room with another bogus complaint, then Health Worry Direct, the new NHS helpline for the sickly, is for you. Simply dial the number and get through straight away to a medical practitioner who will take your initial worry and inflate it into a public health crisis, for which the only cure is lifelong house arrest and confiscation of your telephone line. You should be careful what you wish for.

It's fitting that every British pensioner should have information about how the NHS works – not least because a senior citizen's topics of conversation traditionally revolve around appalling medical conditions, and how many of their friends have recently died just to spite them.

Indeed, when not holidaying in dismal seaside towns or helping out at the local charity shop, most pensioners like nothing better than a cheery day in a hospital corridor discussing their rheumatoid arthritis and bowel movements with a complete stranger, shortly followed by their consultation with the doctor.

But, it's not just old folk who use health services. In fact, a pensioner often ends up in a hospital waiting room full of younger people, none of whom are in the least bit interested in how they've had a slight limp ever since their leg was doodlebugged in the war.

So the Department of Social Scrutiny has compiled this section for pensioners and the living alike. It aims to guide Britons through the maze that is the National Health Service. The following pages are full of hints and tips on everything from the GP's waiting room to major surgery. You will find that this section contains almost everything you need to know to help you get the most out of the NHS. Your NHS.*

---

* Please note, it is not really *your* NHS, and you should avoid turning up willy-nilly to your local hospital and taking the CAT scanner to pieces to claim your share.

> **It may be some time before you can see your doctor, so try to book your appointment before you become ill.**

Booking an appointment

You cannot just walk into your GP's surgery and expect to see a doctor straight away. Instead, you must make an appointment to see your GP for which you will need to talk to an efficient and unflappable medical receptionist who will not be cajoled, amused or flirted with, and who gives the impression that they are saving all their smiles up for something special, such as the first time they get to eat a badger or beat a dormouse to death with an adjustable spanner.

It may be some time until your appointment comes around

Your doctor is busy, and it may be some time before there is a spare appointment for you to see them. For this reason, it is good practice to try to book your appointment before you become ill, in order that your doctor can diagnose your sickness at first hand.

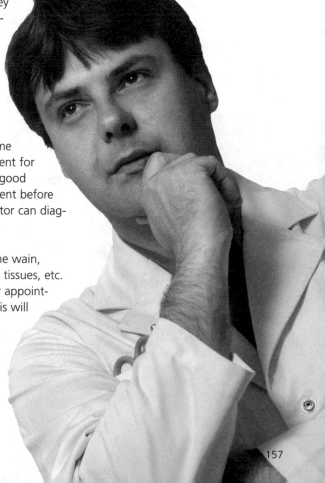

If it seems that your illness is on the wain, collect relevant samples – urine, stool, tissues, etc. Label them all and bring them to your appointment in a supermarket carrier bag. This will give your doctor the chance to diagnose your problem, which, after all, is the fun and challenging part of being a doctor.

Medical Advances

Memory transplant
Neurologists can now confidently pinpont the exact location of memories in the brain and pinch them out with tweezers. Meanwhile, scientists working on transplant technology are experimenting with replacement media and are currently trying to find ways of instilling lemon blancmange with happy memories.

Rectectomy
Removal of a troublesome anus is sometimes the only way to eradicate haemorrhoids completely. Following the operation, patients are "hard-wired" into the sewerage system with a long flexible hose that terminates in an adapter that fits over the waste water inspection cover in your garden.

Above: Try not to swallow medical equipment, as it is security tagged and the NHS always prosecutes thieves.

Give your doctor plenty of information
Your doctor is trained at listening, but it's good manners to try to not monopolise the conversation too much. Ask them how they've been feeling lately because, like most medical staff, your GP may have their own problems.

Your referral to see a specialist
Once your GP has performed a diagnosis, they may become bored and restless and refer you to a specialist at a local hospital.

Whereas your GP is in the frontline of health delivery and deals with people all the time, you may find that a specialist or consultant is a little ethereal and high-handed. As a general rule, consultant surgeons are bad with people but good with knives and golf clubs, which is just about the right attitude to cultivate when you are trained to stab people in a controlled manner. It also helps them to cut through all the small talk and get on with poking large, chromium-plated objects into your body in a somewhat insulting fashion.

Inpatient or outpatient?
These days, with shorter recovery times, there is practically no difference between the two. One hospital in the south west actually performs short operations on the drive back to your home, making a detour if there are any complications on the way.

Your operation
With advances in medicines and procedures, you can come in for a lung or kidney transplant in the morning and be back at work making a presentation by the afternoon (*opposite*). You may feel some sharp stabbing pains in the back, however, and for this we recommend finding a less vindictive place to work.

> **Try not to monopolise the conversation too much. Medical staff have their own problems.**

Your convalescence

Major operations – especially reconstructive cosmetic procedures such as complete torso replacements, installation of washboard abdomens, or removal of the anus – require a long convalescence, and you should avoid using your new body part for a week or two. For most procedures, however, medical advances have meant a return to basic British values of being able to get on with life without too much fuss. In that way at least, the National Health Service is an important part of the nation's fabric.

Help with your Hospital Admission

The Department of Social Scrutiny believes that every patient of the National Health Service should have access to the highest quality medical care, free at the point of use. Just not free.

In pursuance of this policy, the Department of Social Scrutiny has embarked on a programme of toll-booth construction at the exits of all British hospitals to collect payment after your treatment is complete. We accept all major cards and can arrange credit facilities, whereby you simply pay for your treatment in weekly installments of imprisonment or community service, depending on the severity and cost of your former illness.

In the event of not being utterly delighted with your treatment, you have a right under the Sale of Goods Act to return any organ transplants in their original packaging within seven (7) days to claim a full refund.

For your enhanced protection, we have also awarded ourselves a brand new Patients' Charter, partly in recognition of the fact that we are the Government, it's our Charter scheme, and we can do what we damn well like with it.

Application for a Hospital Bed

- The National Health Service is managed dynamically from day-to-day, and you need to complete this form in advance so we can arrange for facilities and equipment to be hired from the local veterinary supplies business. Failure to fill in this form before your arrival in hospital may lead to your operation being performed on a hostess trolley.

- If you are on any courses of medication, you must bring these in with you. This will help our junior doctors to mix and match a range of sedatives and stimulants to control their dizzy spells and hallucinations over a long shift.

Your Name
If you have lost your name, you can apply
for a new identity through your local chapter
of Al Qaeda.

Are you on any medication?

☐ No. I do not believe that breathing deeply and listening to my heart beat will help me.

☐ I have no need for medication as I have a perfectly serviceable stiff upper lip.

Are you interested in our executive service?

☐ Yes. Please add vodka martinis to my intravenous drip.

Last Christmas I gave you my heart

☐ But the very next day you gave it away to the Organ Transplant Authority.

Please order your hospital food here

☐ Grey slop.

Please tick this box if you do not wish to be resuscitated after the chicken pie

☐ I do not wish to be resuscitated to take my chances with pudding, thank you.

Tick if you wish a doctor to scare the living daylights out of your ungrateful family

☐ Yes, please issue a pessimistic prognosis.

Please sign the declaration

I declare that I am legally unwell, and consent
to being patronized and violated by consultants
and passed around the National Health Service
in a spirit of impersonal scientific enquiry.

SOCIAL SCRUTINY

Expiry

PASSING YOUR BEST BEFORE DATE

CONTENTS

A British Life Revisited

A flipbook reconstruction of it flashing before your eyes

404 Error

This page cannot be found

An error has occurred because of a government conspiracy to conceal the truth from you. You may have followed an out-of-date index entry or been referred here by another book but, either way, you have not been feeling well recently, and your continual insistence that this page used to be here will slowly tear you away from your mooring in the harbour of consensus reality.

Please move along
There is nothing to see here. In case of further reality mismatch, please phone our Customer Service Team, which will be happy to freak you out even more.

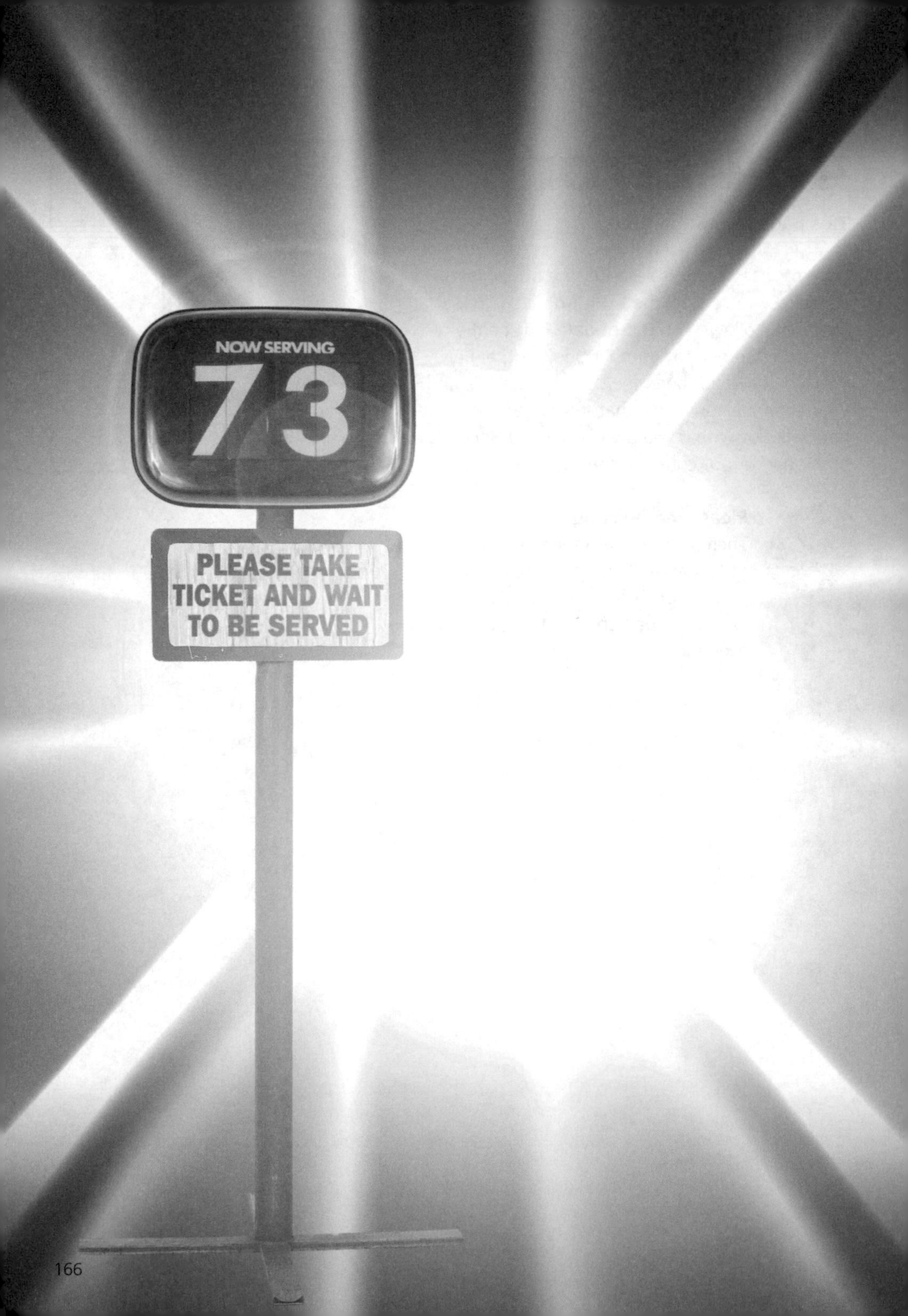
NOW SERVING
73
PLEASE TAKE
TICKET AND WAIT
TO BE SERVED

Welcome to "Death"

So you are dead. Don't bust a gut about it, unless that's how you got here, in which case you'll find some mops and buckets behind reception. Just because you've passed behind the veil of all your tomorrows, doesn't mean to say you have to make the place look untidy.

Before we lead you into your In Felicity Benefit claimant's interview, we would ask you to take a numbered ticket from the dispenser and wait to be called. Remember, this is the United Kingdom of Heaven and you should not try to jump the queue. This applies equally to former OAPs. Don't try that "but I'm only a pensioner" look with us, most of us have had a bad day. Anyone disobeying this command will be severely tutted at.

Once you are called, you must tell us everything about not only your current personal circumstances – which, let's face it with you being dead, are really quite simple – but also about your past circumstances. Don't forget that we have an even more comprehensive overview of your life here than we do in life. We know all about you, even your dirty little secrets. Think of us as being a little bit like an Internet service provider, only for your life, not your broadband connection.

Finally – in more ways than one – welcome to the United Kingdom of Heaven. If you have any questions, please realize, as in life, we have plenty of questions too.

British Heaven

The United Kingdom of Heaven is a unique gated community set in the perfect rolling British countryside of Elysian Fields.

With its opulent surroundings, superior finishes and first-class security system, it is a revelation in comfort and joy. British Heaven is designed by Laurence Llewelyn-Bowen, in collaboration with God.

If you don't believe us, come and see our Near-Death Experience Show Home and you'll see that it's not just the light that's blinding, everything oozes quality, right down to the full-size Moses swimming pool, fed by the River Styx and complete with its own Fountain of Truth.

But hurry, places are limited to a first-come, first-saved basis.

Application for Death

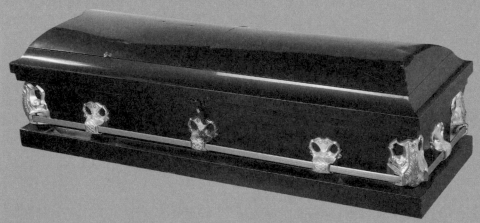

As you would expect, your death creates a lot of important paperwork. This is because, even after you die, the Department of Social Scrutiny continues to work for you and may require information in order to help us help you help us.

This enables us to discharge certain formal duties in much the same way as you have recently discharged yourself. These duties have been sparked off by your death.

By "death", we mean an eternal state of involuntary stillness. It commences with the visit of an anachronistic simile that alludes to a harvest – the Grim Reaper – and leads to either a blinding white light and a withered and rather embarrassed God, reincarnation or absolutely nothing at all.

In the case of reincarnation, even into a lower being such as a dung beetle, journalist or equivalent, you will be asked to repay immediately any In Felicity Benefit you may have claimed, by means of a direct debit by your karmic account bank manager.

In the case of arriving at nothing at all, please make sure you extinguish the blinding white light behind you so as not to disturb others who wish to continue not existing.

In case of finding a benevolent God, you may wish to raise some issues with It, after which you will be asked to fill out the form opposite and await the decision of the claimant advisor.

If you do not agree with the decision, you can appeal against it, using our Claimants' Seance Procedure. Please make your presence felt at a DoSS office, and we will send all the details you need to your book of remembrance.

In Felicity Benefit Claim Form

- Please complete this form in automatic handwriting across the kitchen wall of a suburban semi-detached house that was built on a Navaho burial ground. If you cannot fill in this form yourself, please find a slightly disturbed pubescent girl to fill it in for you.

- Please answer all the questions as fully as your spirit guides will let you. One rap for yes, two raps for no and a 1m-long prominence of ectoplasm for "not applicable". You may also manipulate a swarm of houseflies or flocks of ravens to spell out your responses in the sky.

- You may only use a fax machine if you are familiar with the protocols required to possess and channel the Hayes command set.

We know your name
We know everything.

How do you know that you are dead?

☐ I remember living in Eastbourne with great affection.

☐ I have become all-knowing, but also now smell a little peculiar.

☐ My back garden appears to have turned into an aerial view of my house.

☐ There are sun beams emanating from my forehead, navel and genital areas.

Did you think you led a good life?

☐ I was a middle manager and nobody ever asked me to think, so no. On both counts.

☐ I confess only to morris dancing and the occasional bit of devil worship.

☐ I paid my taxes on time, always filled in official forms correctly and never lost my temper with a government department, so there is probably something a little unnatural about me.

Please sign the declaration

I declare that I am dead and will remain so until I have been notified otherwise by the Department of the Great Wheel of Life. I agree not to bother the living or I will be threatened with an anti-social behaviour order, full ritual exorcism or an eternal recording of the rock group Genesis. This is my claim for In Felicity Benefit, Amen.

Sign

Date

And Another Thing...
APPENDICES

CONTENTS

"Always leave 'em wanting more or, at least stop before the restraining orders."
Devonian aphorism

Please ... NTALS using
piece ... you do no[t]
kno[w] ... ea. The
judg[e]

Tick boxes ...

Do NOT ... Lapsed Clergy   This isn't the ... CofE Archbishop

Cliff Richard   Smart Fridge

Your name   Tony Blair   God

Do you have a partner?   Yes   Please send us some of their skin.

No ... ...ological inability to trust others on a separate sheet.

May we look in your dustbin?   Yes   We will return in a suspect-looking boiler sui[t]
We need to do this in order to
freak you out.

Do you have children?   No   What have you done with them?

Yes ... following question:

What is their total weight in bushels?   Bushel[s]
We need to know this in order to cause you
as much trouble as possible.

Would you care for an older relative?   No   Thanks, I've just p[ut on]e

Yes   Please answer the following question:

Please estimate their calorific value   Kilojoule[s]

Do you find this form confusing in any way?   9. See 12 Across (4,3

Please tick if you wish to be cloned.   We will issue duplicate cards and partner[s]

# Secure Data Policy

Naturally, with all the personal information and data the Department of Social Scrutiny have to collect about you, you'd expect us to operate a rock-solid Information Security Policy and to treat all your personal details with the utmost respect. What we can promise you, however, is that we really try our best and, if we make a mistake, we will come straight out and admit it after a brief cooling-off period, a public enquiry and some hurtful insinuations about your honesty from our expertly trained attack lawyers.

That said, your information is almost always safe at the DoSS state-of-the-art data centre.

The perimeter gate is manned by staff wearing fancy dress police uniform and expressions of hateful melancholy that put off authorized visitors, let alone trespassers.

Even if trespassers wriggle their way past the perimeter guards, with their 24-hour CCTV and Sky Sports monitoring, they will still have to face the DoSS Datashield – an obfuscatory computer system so unfriendly and frustrating to use, only Zen masters can resist the temptation to smash it to pieces with a stick. Adepts are trained for six months to penetrate the Datashield, and can only endure a year of work with it before they are de-programmed in a DoSS bunker in Worthing that will enable them to lead a normal life again, but will unfortunately spoil their memories of Worthing for ever.

Information kills
This data card could be lethal, if applied with enough force and determination.

Other DoSS Forms

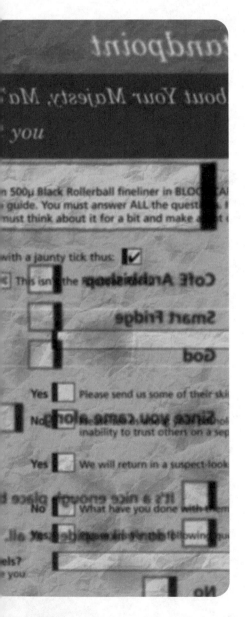

Application to find your car keys
Form K4rK3y5
An emergency procedure when patting your pockets, looking under the cat that looks a little too pleased with itself and, when Googling for "car key" AND "mine" AND "please" does not turn up anything useful – except for some mildly distracting pornography.
Warning: *This form calls out a search party, which will tear your home apart in a relentless search that becomes logarhythmically more unreasonable with every passing moment.*

Application to apply for an application form
Form A²
A gateway order form to obtain the form of your choice. To order this form, you must first complete an order form order form.

DoSS job application form
Please wait for two weeks after the deadline to find out if you have got the job. DoSS regularly communicates with its agents in the field via messages left in their household refuse. If you have not thought of going through your bin for secret mail from the government, then we're sorry, you are simply too mentally stable to work for us. Thank you for your interest.

Biometrics exemption certificate application
A simple one-page form for people with no face, fingerprints or DNA who may later turn out to be some kind of non-biological material that is deceptively person-shaped. We have printed over 10 million of these forms, and expect some delays in processing the applications.

DoSS Publications

The Department of Social Scrutiny publishes many useful leaflets written in easy to digest, bite-sized chunks that carefully explain the law in lay-person's terms. We then lock them away in gun-metal filing cabinets as if our lives depended upon it. Here are a couple of the other ones.

Biopassport

DOSSBEPI, the new DoSS Biometrically Enhanced Passport Initiative, goes hand-in-hand with our new programme of National Identity Card forehead barcoding, electronic tagging and 24-hour surveillance monitoring from that house across the street, where shadowy figures with army-issue binoculars and recording equipment may or may not lurk in dim pools of light barely perceptible through the slats of half-cocked Venetian blinds. It's nothing to worry about, honest.

Biscuits

Biscuits, an authoritarian guide is the new leaflet from DoSS that outlines the exact tendering requirements when contracting out the supply of biscuits, cakes and other ambient-temperature, hand-held casual snacks for government agencies and departments.

Measurements of absorbency and thermo-dynamic response are all stipulated, as are the recommended cup diameters for most major British biscuits.

Contact DoSS

At DoSS, we are always interested in your opinions and would normally just log them automatically via your phone and email as well as microphones attached to the back of your fridge and the rectum of your dog *(reception diagram, left)*.

However, if you really feel you need to contact us, just leave a note on the windscreen of the unmarked Transit van parked at the end of your road for the last week. If the matter is urgent, we suggest you shout "Bin Laden" during the course of any UK phone call, and a small group of our representatives will call on you in the early hours of Sunday morning.

Contacting Us By Post

You can contact us via Her Majesty's Electric Post Office at the following address:

Department of Social Scrutiny
Interrogation Room 487
Golden Cross House
456-458 Strand
London
WC2R 0DZ

Please enclose a stamped addressed envelope if you wish to receive a reply in 18 months' time.

Contacting Us By Email

Since last year, the government has been actively working in a public–private partnership to facilitate a forward-looking policy of instituting inclusive and bilateral electronic communications. We hope to be able to collect our email by 2010.

We may use any information you give us for the purposes of oppressing you. We may share your information with carefully selected intelligence networks and the armed forces.

Index

D

darkness, moments of 28
death, application for 168–9
decimal music 38
decision making 132–5
deconstruction 65 (lard)
democracy, British 126, 132, 133 (with
reference to edible rice paper)
Department of Motion (DOMO) 83
Department of Social Scrutiny (DOSS) 6, 33,
43, 57, 64, 65, 73, 76, 129, 153, 156
DOSS Forms 174
DOSS Publications 175
Diet, British National 57, 64–5
dinner, evening, being served at traffic
junctions 85
doctor's dizzy spells 161
dodgy payments *see democracy*
dogs, not to be confused with children 47
Domesday Book, publication of 32
dominoes 79
Doonican, Val 2, 36
driver, bus 96
duel 2

E

eating, healthy 71
edible rice paper *see dodgy payments*
education 47, 48–9 (including traffic
cones) *see also schools*
ego and id *see drivers, bus*
elderly men, parallels with British
constitution 127
Election Night 127
embezzlement (British) 133
emergency rail map 94–5
Emergency Services 39,
see also Park 'n' Bleed
emotional nonsense *see obsession*
Eternal Moment of Danger 129

European Court of Human Rights
see teatime
Evil, Combined Forces of 138
Exeter, telephone directory *see education*

F

Fare Dodger Electrode Harpoon 97
feng shui, as storage system 14
fetishism, fiscal 116
fish fingers 66–7
flakiness *see paranoia*
Fleming, Alexander 43 (brains)
flick knives 49 (comprehensive schools)
food
convenience 66
foreign and subversive 57
the worse it tastes, the healthier it is 72
frying, deep-fat see Diet, British National
fuck, what the *see tax*

G

geophysics, the dullness of 24
Germans, attempted invasion
see Royal Family
gift tokens 22
Glastonbury 30
grandchildren, best ways to threaten 148
gravy
jump-starting migraines 50
solidifying 50
Greyday Bus Pass 96
Grim Reaper 168–9
guard dog 146

H

Habeus Corpus 127, 129
Hadrian's Wall 30
haemorrhoids, as opening gambit in
chatting up an OAP 149
hags, East End 57

O

obsession *see weather*

offal, putrid and disgusting *see school dinners*

offspring, and weight in bushels 12

older relatives, and calorific value 12

Open University, compulsory viewing 11

oral pleasure 62 (nothing to do with the French)

organ-transplant
    payment of 160
    sale and return 160
    thieves 146

P

paranoia, and flakiness 9

Park 'n' Bleed 39

Pensioner Appraisal Programme 148

Personal Equity Plan 105

personal missiles 87

pied wagtails *see retirement*

pocket-sized hound 154

poo, as liquidized slop 43

post-structuralism 65 (tartar sauce)

pottering and getting on people's nerves *see retirement*

psychiatrically challenged 9

psychometric questions 136

pub games, and the sound of broken windows 78, 79

public house 76–9

Q

Queen, as German (indisputably)

R

rail travel
    the infrastructure
    a) get real, and b) saving up to buy tickets 90–3

impenetrable signalling system 91

dodgy scraping noises 93

see also sincere apology system, automated

Rail Tsar 83

rectectomy 159

reggae *see serf assessment*

repossessions (easily arranged) 120

Restoration, the 34

rhinoceros, dead 7

road signs explained 88–9

roads, in four flavours, new and useless 84

Romans (Can you imagine how long it would take to drive to Guilford if they hadn't invaded?) 83

roof aerials 139

Royal Family
    dead pheasants 16
    gaffs per mile 36
    lickspittle 16
    serfs and nobs 17

Royal Navy, parking 22

rum-tiddly-tum music 144

S

saliva 66

Satanism 2

Saxons 30

school dinners 50–1

school timetable 52–3

schools
    as breeding ground for liars 48
    impossibility of getting children into 47

self-employment 104

self-importance, being British 11

sensory deprivation *see school dinners and cold, uptight, arrogant, insensitive, patronising Frenchmen*

serf assessment 8–9

serfs and nobs *see Royal Family*

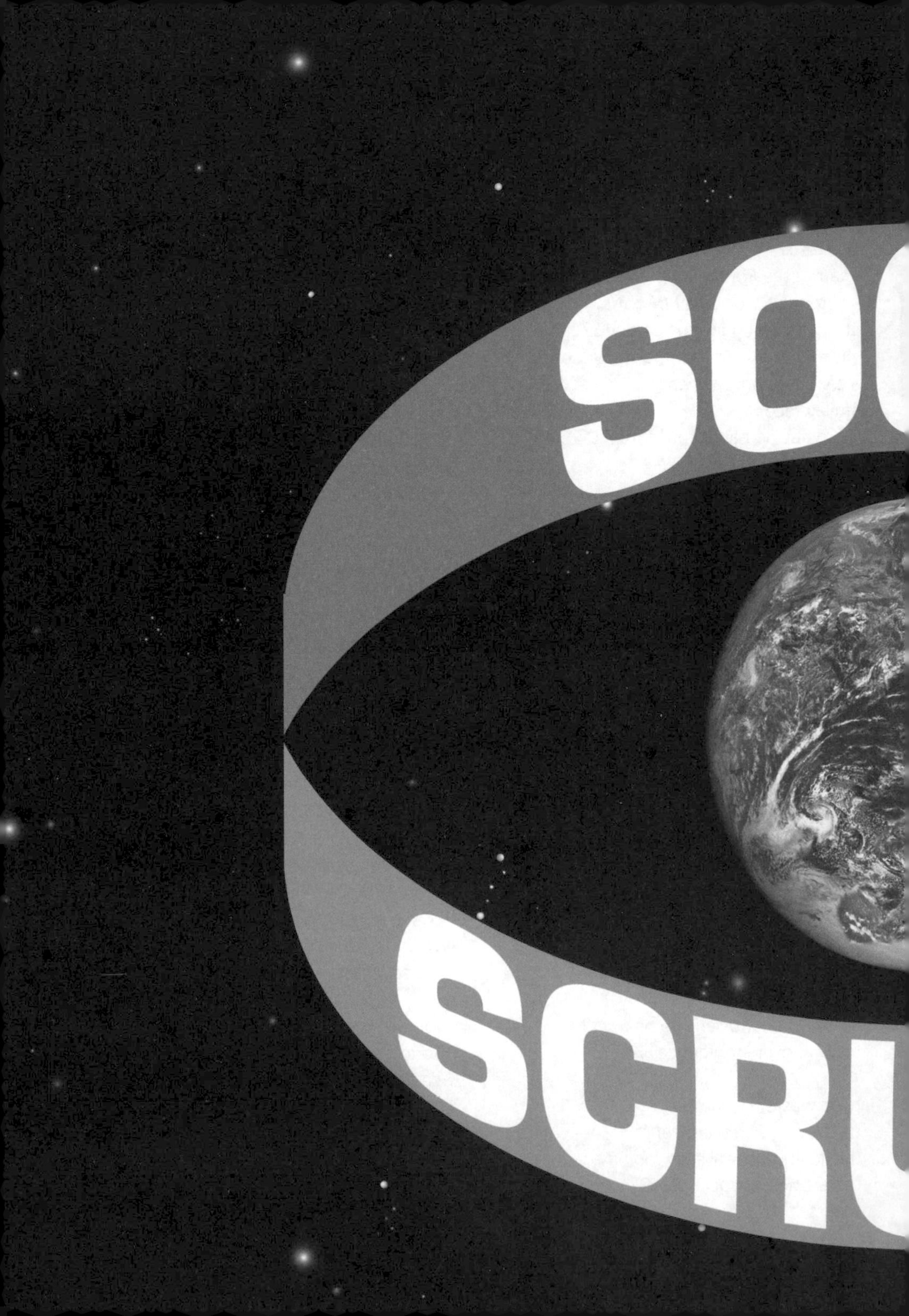

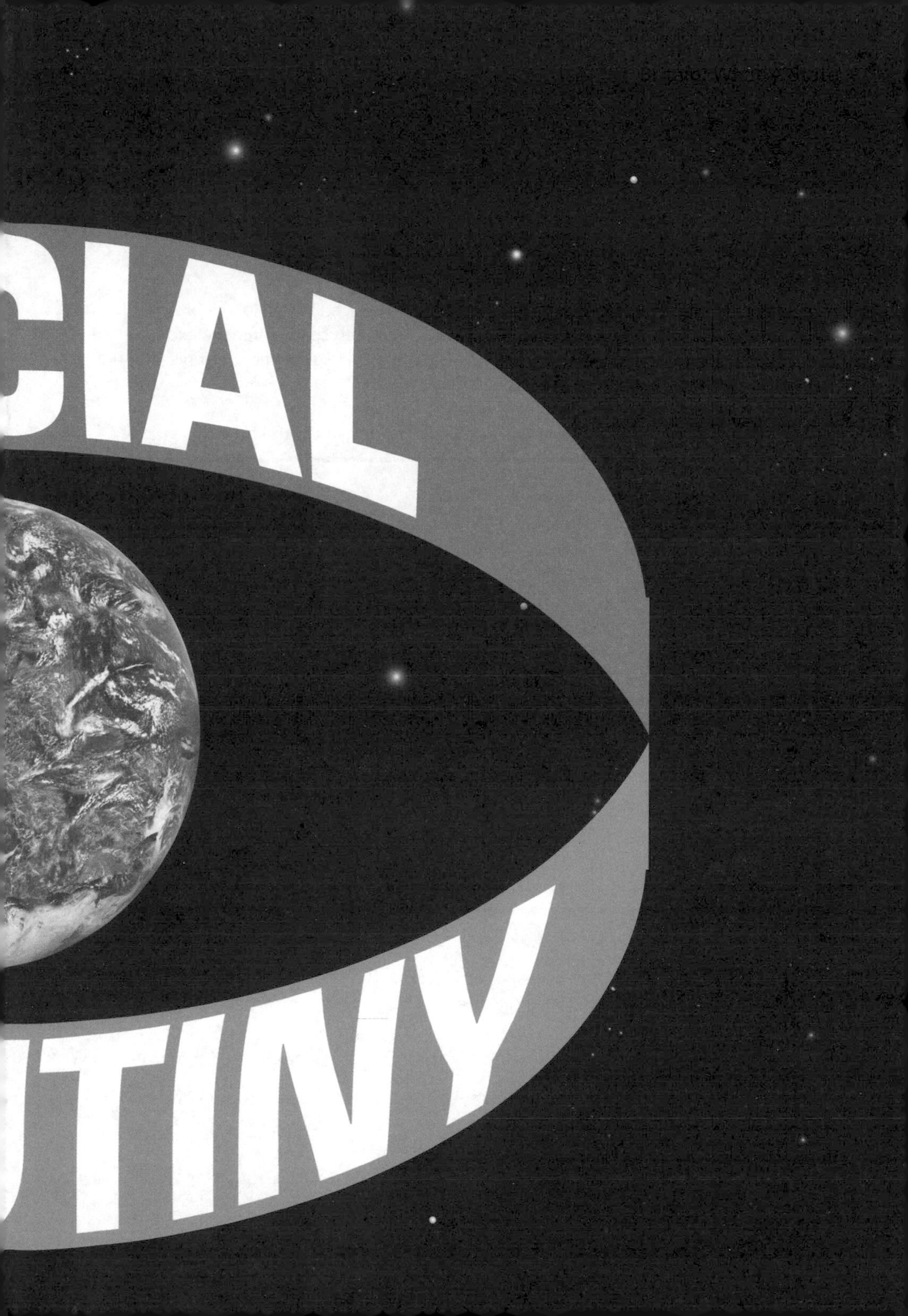
CIAL
TINY

For Office Use Only

- This section is in black and white so that we can promote a mood of monochrome austerity in order to reassure you that the Taxpayer's money is being well spent.

- This form is Government property. While most of the preceding 183 pages are classified as Public Rights of Way that you are free to wander over, this space is for the exclusive use – and where applicable, enjoyment – of this office, and the Government reserves the right to chase you off with guns if you trespass upon it.

- Please do not mark below this line or we will come after you with knives.

☐ 9"   ☐ Pepperoni   ☐ Deep pan

☐ 12"   ☐ Garlic   ■ Urgent

☐ Latte   ☐ Cappuccino   ☐ Caffeine-laced loony juice

The Chord of C Minor   Velociraptor

Please do not mark below this line as we need somewhere to put our doughnuts while we work on your claim

☐ TCP-IP   ☐ Prep-H   Further Notes

☐ DYSWIDT   ☐ AK-47   Can we send one of our
                              "TV License Detector Vans" arou
☐ C3PO   ☐ QWERTY   to this one:

☐ DEATH   ☐ TTFN